Selected Poems of Isabella Andreini

Edited and with an introduction by
Anne MacNeil
Translation with annotations by
James Wyatt Cook

The Scarecrow Press, Inc.
Lanham, Maryland • Toronto • Oxford
2005

SCARECROW PRESS, INC.

Published in the United States of America
by Scarecrow Press, Inc.
A wholly owned subsidiary of
The Rowman & Littlefield Publishing Group, Inc.
4501 Forbes Boulevard, Suite 200, Lanham, Maryland 20706
www.scarecrowpress.com

PO Box 317
Oxford
OX2 9RU, UK

British Library Cataloguing in Publication Information Available

Library of Congress Cataloging-in-Publication Data
Andreini, Isabella, 1562–1604.
  [Poems. English & Italian. Selections]
  Selected poems of Isabella Andreini / edited and with an introduction by Anne
MacNeil ; translation with annotations by James Wyatt Cook.
     p. cm.
  Text of poems in English and Italian.
  Includes bibliographical references and index.
  ISBN 0-8108-5442-2 (pbk. : alk. paper)
  1. Andreini, Isabella, 1562–1604—Translations into English. I. MacNeil,
Anne. II. Cook, James Wyatt, 1932– III. Title.
  PQ4562.A72A26 2005
  851'.5—dc22
                                                                    2004031095

Queste traduzioni sono dedicate
alla memoria onorata
della Signora
Alberta Cuoghi Polucci

Contents

Editor's Foreword   vii
Translator's Foreword   ix

1   Introduction   1
2   Selections from *Rime d'Isabella Andreini Padovana, comica gelosa* (1601)   29
3   Selections from *Rime d'Isabella Andreini comica gelosa, & academica intenta detta l'Accesa. Parte seconda* (1605)   165

Index of First Lines   211
About the Editor and Translator   215

Editor's Foreword

In the decade since I first started writing on the life and works of Isabella Andreini, scholarly attention to this influential figure in the history of Renaissance theater has happily bloomed. The intervening years have produced critical editions of her pastoral play, *Mirtilla*, in both Italian and English, a number of anthologies of Italian literature and women's writings in which Andreini's poems appear, and an ever-widening field of critiques of her contributions to Renaissance drama. As a result, Andreini's works are fast becoming a mainstay of classroom study, forming a critical link between the pastoral dramas of Torquato Tasso and Battista Guarini and providing an important early seventeenth-century oasis of women's lyric poetry after Gaspara Stampa and Vittoria Colonna.

This volume seeks to present a broad cross-section of Andreini's lyric poetry, both in its original language and in the fine verse translations of James Wyatt Cook. This is the first edition of a substantial number of Andreini's poems in English. In selecting the poems for inclusion in this volume, I have considered the range of Andreini's style, the diversity of genres in which she composed, her commentaries on Renaissance court society, and her interactions with other poets and patrons of the late sixteenth century. My aim in the introduction is to provide a cultural and historical foundation which will, in turn, deepen the reader's understanding of Andreini and her poems. There is much work to be done in the study of Isabella Andreini and her family, and I can only hope that the present volume will inspire future translations and publications of Andreini's *Lettere*, her *Fragmenti d'alcune scritture*, and the remaining lion's share of her lyric poetry.

This project had its beginnings over a decade ago on the main quad of the University of Chicago. I am indebted to the bold scholars there who encouraged me to pursue my study of Isabella Andreini, even when my research led outside the traditional boundaries of my field. Most profoundly, I am indebted to the well-loved and highly esteemed late Howard Mayer Brown, who first recommended Andreini as a focus of investigation. Howard's influence over this book runs deep. He once told me that the book designer Robert Williams was the first person at Chicago ever to talk to him, and I, too, have found in Bob a wise and faithful friend. He was the first to urge me to take up the edition and translation of Andreini's lyric poems, and for this I owe him many thanks. Howard also recommended my work to the editor Bruce Phillips, who has overseen publication of both my *Music and Women of the Commedia dell'Arte in the Late Sixteenth Century* for Oxford University Press and this volume of Andreini's lyric poems for Scarecrow Press. Bruce is a brilliant editor, whose guidance has helped shape the musicological literature of recent decades. Howard further introduced me to the incomparable scholar Elissa Weaver, who in turn recommended my collaborator, James Wyatt Cook, to me and performed all necessary introductions. To Jim I owe an unfathomable well of gratitude for the patient support with which he buoyed this project over the years of its inception. He is both code breaker and poet—the very best combination for illuminating the wiles of a crafty comedienne.

Anne MacNeil
Fellow of the American Academy in Rome
University of North Carolina at Chapel Hill

Translator's Foreword

For someone coming to Isabella Andreini's lyrics from the verse of her literary forebears, a first impression may well focus equally on her mastery of Renaissance Italian poetic idiom and on the derivative qualities of her poems. By emulating the genres, the diction, and often the metaphors of the lyricists who preceded her, particularly Petrarch, she simultaneously asserts her place in the canon of vernacular Italian lyric and, as she also does in her letters, acknowledges her debts to her predecessors. Her devotion to Petrarch appears in her employment of many of his favorite forms: sonnet, madrigal, and sestina. Her close acquaintance with his lyrics reveals itself as well in her deployment of Petrarchan lines to construct centos on themes of her own, as she does in her first cento (Centone I), one of three poems mourning the death of her friend Laura Guidiccioni Lucchesini. Andreini's selecting Petrarch's lines to express her personal grief, it seems, establishes enough emotional distance from her loss that she can "give sorrow tongue."

Similarly, in her first *capitolo*, "Lunghe da le tue luci alme, e divine" ("Far distant from your kindly, heavenly eyes"), she takes every third line from Petrarch and embeds it in a *terza-rima* stanza—the verse form of the *Divina Commedia*—thereby paying simultaneous tribute to Petrarch and to Dante. Likewise, her fondness for *scherzi* and pastorals invoke the lyric practice of Tasso and Boiardo.

Her principal innovation as a lyricist, perhaps, appears when she adopts both male and female personae and points of view in her poems. With respect to earlier Italian lyric verse, this androgyny of poetic voice seems to be her particular contribution. She carefully points it out as a carryover from her stage experience in the first of her sonnets: "And, as in theaters, in varied style, / I now have played a woman, now a man / So in green April, following once more / My star of fleeting years, With varied style / I ruled lines for at least a thousand leaves" (Sonnet 1, ll. 9–14). Her care in highlighting this practice suggests that she did consider it a noteworthy departure from the practice of earlier Italian vernacular poets. Madrigals 13, 18, and 36 are among the poems that illustrate this poetic strategy.

As one who has also translated Petrarch, I was particularly struck by Andreini's greater willingness to subordinate her literary agendas to personal, religious, and social ones. Petrarch's love of Laura and his unflagging pursuit of literary fame—even at the risk of certainty concerning the state of his soul—leaves him forever wandering in a spiritual labyrinth. Conversely, Andreini's deep commitment to Roman Catholic doctrine and to the Counter-Reformation positions of her contemporary church, her admiration for Cardinal San Giorgio Cinthio Aldobrandini (to whom she dedicated her *Rime*), and her adherence to a fairly rigid code of conventional personal morality appear prominently in her verse and in her letters. Doubts on the subject of religious matters seem seldom to have afflicted her. Although she employs in many poems the conventions of Italian vernacular love lyric and complains of Love's tyranny and its consequent woe, in Sonnet 159 and elsewhere she rejects the amorous literary tradition and asserts Christian happiness in its place. A series of spiritual poems confirms her devotion to Roman Catholic values. Similarly, in *Egloga* 3, though she reveals a surprising knowledge of spells and witchcraft, she rejects superstition and asserts conventional religion and common sense.

In her poems, other personal qualities, like her classical erudition, appear as well. Particularly in her epistolary sonnets, like the one responding to Angelo Ingegneri's criticism of the artificiality of one of her stage performances, we find evidence of her wit, her self-respect both as artist and woman, her skill at verbal fencing and sarcastic repartee, and her quick intelligence. Exchanging letters in sonnet form was very much in vogue among the intelligentsia and literati of Andreini's Europe. Several examples of her responses, together with the sonnets written by others that she answered, appear here. In their texts one can trace her careful analysis of her correspondents' intentions and motives as well as the courtesy and urbanity of her manners. Above all, they reveal her as a woman at the very pinnacle of artistic fame, and they document the acceptance of her preeminence both by artists and intellectuals and by the crowned and titled luminaries of royal and noble Europe.

Her capacity for friendship also appears in several of her poems, particularly those on the death of Laura Guidiccioni Lucchesini. We see as well the emotional depth of her response to performance and her admiration for her artistic peers in a poem (*canzonetta morale* 9) praising Ottavio Rinuccini's version of an early opera, *Euridice*. This poem I found particularly interesting because, while it celebrated the artist and his libretto, it also served as a critical *repris* and review. In sonnet 119, Andreini employs the shorter form to a similar purpose.

The volumes from which I have translated these selections are *Rime D'Isabella Andreini Padovana, Comica Gelosa* and *Rime D'Isabella Andreini Comica Gelosa & Academica Intenta detta l'Accesa*, Part 2, Milan: Girolamo Bordone & Pietromartire Locarni, 1601 and 1605, respectively—the first printed editions of Andreini's collected lyrics. As has been my usual practice when translating from rhymed Italian verse, I have chosen to approximate the Italian original with English blank verse that, while rendering the Italian very literally, strives to reflect the tone and nuance of the original in the English simulacrum. This practice has produced a diction that feels to me broadly modern, though it does occasionally produce verb-noun and noun-adjective inversions that may strike some as archaic. In my view, however, such inversions are legitimate resources for writers working in fixed forms. Although I have sacrificed rhyme in general, I have made no effort to suppress accidental rhyme when it occurs.

The selection printed here represents a fair sample of the subjects and variety in the entire corpus of Andreini's lyrics. In presenting the Italian versions, I have very lightly edited Andreini's original text, principally supplying dropped letters, line numbers, and Italian quotation marks. I have not modernized Andreini's spellings or accentual system, so that "h" appears frequently in situations where modern Italian does not employ it, and accents are also archaic. None of this archaism, however, should interfere with reading the Italian text if one is conversant with contemporary Italian. For those who may not be accustomed to pronouncing Italian verse, the Italian metrical line is regularly achieved by eliding adjacent vowels and semivowels. Thus, "*egli è uno huomo*" would be pronounced as four syllables: "*egl'un'uomo*," with the "gl" pronounced approximately like the "ll" in English "million."

I am grateful to Anne MacNeil for her patient and good-humored collaboration, for her scholarly acumen, for her choice of poems to include here, and for her unflagging good cheer in the face of an improbable and unfortunate adversity that delayed this publication by almost five years. I also wish to thank my dear spouse, Barbara Collier Cook, for her help in preparing the manuscript and for her unswerving support and encouragement. Thanks finally to Konrad Eisenbichler of the University of Toronto for double-checking the accuracy of my translation against the Italian and to Elissa Weaver for having suggested the project to me in the first place.

James Wyatt Cook
Langbo Trustees' Professor Emeritus, Albion College

Chapter 1
Introduction

Nearly all of Andreini's lyric poetry is contained in two volumes of *Rime*, first published in 1601 and 1605, respectively, and dedicated to Cardinal Cinzio Aldobrandini of Rome. Both were quite popular *canzonieri* in Italy and in France, and copies of them tend to show up in the libraries of noble men and women in the early years of the seventeenth century. The first volume was put to press by Andreini with the Milanese publishers Girolamo Bordone and Pietromartire Locarni and is prefaced by a single dedicatory poem by Erycius Puteanus, doctor of classical languages at the Palatine University in Milan and a student of the Belgian scholar Justus Lipsius. The second edition of this first book of *Rime* was published in Paris in 1603, while Andreini was in residence at the French royal court. The third edition, printed in Italy in 1605, together with the first edition of Andreini's *Rime . . . parte seconda* and her pastoral play, *Mirtilla*, was published as a commemorative volume following the actress's death at Lyons in 1604. It includes many added dedicatory verses, in both Latin and Italian, from Puteanus, Antonio Maria Spelta, Angelo Ingegneri, Ottavio Rinuccini, Giovan Battista Marino, and Gherardo Borgogni, among others. Most of these encomiums were written on the occasion of Andreini's passing (she died in childbirth at the age of forty-two), and the edition itself serves as a memorial to its author's lifelong dedication to the literary arts.

Andreini's two volumes of *Rime* encompass nearly five hundred lyric poems. In addition, she wrote a pastoral play, *Mirtilla*, first published in 1588, roughly one hundred dramatic monologues, or *Lettere* (1607), and a volume of theatrical dialogues and other dramatic scenes (*Fragmenti d'alcune scritture*, 1620). The bulk of Andreini's poems are composed in the forms of sonnet, madrigal, *canzonetta* (or *scherzo*), and tercet. Her verses are noteworthy for their conscious use of modeling, either of a specfic precursor or of another writer's style. Such modeling often relates to the subject matter of the poem as well as to its form and style, as when Andreini quotes Petrarch in her funeral verses for Laura Guidiccioni Lucchesini, thus drawing a parallel between Petrarch's Laura and her own.

Andreini's compositional style emphasizes imagery, comprehensive form, and rhetorical twists of language. Her madrigals invoke a Petrarchan manner filled with pastoral allegories, whereas her *scherzi* generally follow the dictates of Chiabreresque meters and rhetorical devices, also centering, however, on pastoral imagery. In these things she is not unlike other poets of the late sixteenth century. Madrigal composition at this time evolves from a largely Petrarchan style toward a Marinist aesthetic, and the lighter poetic forms, such as the *scherzo*, *canzonetta*, and *villanesca*, are highly influenced by French style, as filtered through the works of Gabriello Chiabrera.

Andreini comes to poetic composition from the perspective of a pragmatist. She is known to have extemporized poems in much the same manner as she improvised dialogue on stage, and she had neither the leisure nor the inclination to compose poems in private, solely for her own enjoyment. Andreini thus occupies a unique niche among late Renaissance literati, in that she embraces the "public" compositional strategies of one who performs on stage, either as an actor or an orator, while eschewing the more intimate manner of most women writers. As a result, many of Andreini's poems have a strong rhetorical cast and a direct simplicity of subject.

During the period when Andreini was preparing her first book of lyric poetry for publication, she exchanged letters with the Belgian scholar Erycius Puteanus, who was then doctor of classical languages at the Palatine School in Milan. In these letters, Puteanus encourages Andreini to continue with her work, entreating her to remember herself to their age through written as well as spoken words, and imploring her to be as fertile in books as she is in children. Andreini's letters in return focus on elucidating the neoclassical precepts underlying friendship, love, stagecraft, and poetic composition.[1]

Andreini's literary persona invokes a male voice, achieved mainly through a masculine gendering of the poems' subjects, but also through humanistic imitation. Her verses are written from a man's point of view and in a forceful literary style associated with men. Questions of gendering, neoclassical imitation, virtue, and rhetoric are broached explicitly in Andreini's correspondence with Puteanus, and these letters have shown that the masculine personification of Andreini's literary works is a conscious construct. Andreini's masculine compositional style is not unique when viewed against a broad spectrum of poetic styles in the late sixteenth century, but it is uncommon among the writings of other female poets of the time, who usually compose in a woman's voice and in a more intimate style. A comparison of Andreini with other women authors shows that her masculine compositional style subverts the female voice and therefore her identity as a woman as well. At the same time, it affords her a wider scope of literary influence and social mobility, which she achieves in scholarly circles and academies. Academies as a rule admitted few women in the sixteenth and seventeenth centuries, but they were accessible to Andreini, if not through membership, as in the case of the Accademia degli Intenti of Pavia, then at least through correspondence, as with the Accademia Filarmonica of Verona and the Accademia Olimpica of Vicenza.

This masculine perspective emerges in nearly all of Andreini's poems. The lovers whose kisses are longed for are nymphs, and descriptive passages dwell on the adored one's rosy, honey-laden lips, her golden hair, her ivory breast. Other women poets of the Renaissance, in contrast, write from a distinctively feminine perspective. Veronica Gambara, Vittoria Colonna, Gaspara Stampa, and Veronica Franco, for example, all write in the female voice, comparing the lovers in their poems with Mars and Adonis, the mythological lovers of Venus. Alternately, some of their poems express highly personal, individualistic sentiments, with the author's husband or lover cast as the object of poetic adoration.[2] Only Laura Terracina, the poet best known for her commentary on Ariosto's *Orlando furioso*, shares with Andreini this propensity for writing from a masculine subject position.

Andreini's first book of *Rime* represents the major part of her compositions in lyric verse. It contains, all together, 359 poems: 197 sonnets, 115 madrigals, 10 *canzonette morali*, 9 each of *scherzi* and *egloghe boschereccie,* and a smattering of other genres, including 2 *sestine,* 2 *epitalami,* 2 *centoni,* 3 *capitoli,* and 4 *versi funerali.* Andreini's dedication offers the publication to Cinzio Aldobrandini, Cardinal San Giorgio and nephew of Pope Clement VIII, as a gift unworthy of his esteem and generosity toward its author.[3]

Included among the poems of the first book are centonizations on verses of Petrarch and encomiums for Ottavio Rinuccini and Gabriello Chiabrera. These poets, together with Torquato Tasso, are among the most important influences on Andreini's style. Petrarchan emulations demonstrate Andreini's adherence to the most widespread trend in sixteenth-century versification, imitation of the sharp imagistic contrasts and introspective mood of the fourteenth-century author's verse.[4] The sonnets appearing early in her *Rime*, and similarly appearing early in the present volume, offer good examples of this youthful, exhuberant style, at which Andreini excels. In these poems, she contrasts a pilgrim's parched, burning thirst with the cooling drops of an Alpine stream, as in "Qual Ruscello veggiam d'acque sovente," and placid breezes with the raging tempests of the sea ("Spirando l'aure placide, e seconde"). More intricately, Andreini molds tender metaphors that draw together the vagaries of love with nature's wilderness. The fragile boat containing a lover's hope breaks up on the rocky shoals of his beloved's disdain, only to sink into an abyss of sorrow in "Spirando l'aure placide, e seconde" and the burgeoning dawn assumes its age-old guise of a nymph's golden hair in the delightfully sad "Le perle già di rugiadoso humore."

Andreini's poems in honor of Chiabrera, in contrast to those which emulate Petrarch, demonstrate a conscious use of neoclassical imitation and rhetorical gesture, characteristics favored at the very end of the century and associated primarily with Chiabrera's work. Of Andreini's three verses for the Ligurian poet, the two *canzonette morali* "Vago di posseder l'indico argento" and "Faccia al gran Marte risonar le 'ncudi" are homages to virtue. She writes these in response to a sonnet Chiabrera penned for her after seeing her perform on stage, probably in Savona in 1584. His poem, "Nel giorno che sublime in bassi manti," praises the actress for her Neoplatonic imitations of the divine madness of poets. In her *canzonette morali*, Andreini returns Chiabrera's praises by implying his own inspiration to divine madness, as well as affirming the bond between the genre of the *canzonetta* and neoclassical conceptions of virtue.

Andreini's other homage to Chiabrera, the scherzo "Ecco l'Alba ruggiadosa," demonstrates her regard for his rejuvenation of the *canzonetta* as a Franco-Italian ideal. The *scherzo* is a markedly different poetic genre than the sonnet, and its literary and aesthetic functions contrast sharply with the older, more studied form. Its antecedent, the *canzonetta*, became popular in Italy during the 1570s and 1580s, although the *scherzo*—a name coined by Chiabrera—came into vogue only in the first thirty years of the seventeenth century.[5] Chiabrera sought to imitate the easy, amorous expression of French poetry in this newly named form. "Do you not take pleasure in seeing such *scherzi* so lovingly represented, which require no effort, nor comment, nor gloss to be understood?"[6]

The form is similar to that of the French *ode*. The French poet and nobleman Pierre de Ronsard had composed neoclassical *odes* during the mid-sixteenth century, and the formal conventions of his verses became standard among the authors of the Plèiade in Paris during the 1570s and 1580s.[7] Chiabrera consciously imitated the form and style of the French neoclassical *ode* as composed by Ronsard in his Italian lyric poems, and he called them *scherzi* to distinguish them from other *canzonette* that did not emulate ancient authorities.[8] Chiabrera's publication of *scherzi* and his treatise, *Le maniere de' versi toscani*, together with the increased Italian and French interaction occasioned by the marriage of Henry IV and Maria de' Medici, brought the new style of French-influenced *scherzo* to the forefront of Italian literary and musical attention in the first years of the seventeenth century. The style Andreini adopts for her own *scherzi*, such as the lovely "Ecco l'Alba ruggiadosa," which is the sole *scherzo* dedicated to Chiabrera in the first printing of her *Rime*,[9] shows an equally ardent attention to simple, straightforward expressions of love and to nature's embodiment of love. Such unaffected verse appealed to musical composers, for Andreini's *scherzi* are among her most often-set lyrics. "Ecco l'Alba ruggiadosa" was given musical settings by Amante Franzoni and Giovanni Ghizzolo, and "Io credèa che tra gli amanti" and "Movèa dolce un zefiretto," both of which are dedicated to Chiabrera in later editions of Andreini's *Rime*, were set to music by Eleuterio Guazzi and Giulio Santo Pietro del Negro, respectively.[10]

Andreini's regard for the simple, unaffected manner characteristic of Chiabrera's work is further shown in her encomiums for Ottavio Rinuccini, for both she and Rinuccini write in an easy, representational style. Rinuccini is best known for composing the poetic texts of important monuments of early music drama. His *Euridice* was set to music by Jacopo Peri and performed at the Florentine court in 1600 for the wedding celebrations of Henry IV of France and Maria de' Medici. Claudio Monteverdi wrote the musical setting for Rinuccini's *Arianna* for the wedding of Francesco Gonzaga and Margherita of Savoy in Mantua in 1608, and Monteverdi also set Rinuccini's *Lamento della Ninfa* to music. It is included in the composer's *Ottavo libro de' madrigali*, published in 1638.[11] Andreini's *canzonetta morale* in honor of Rinuccini, "Ove tra vaghi fior nascosto è l'Angue," with its accompanying remark, "How marvelous is the power of poetry," focuses on the plot and

composition of *Euridice*, offering only in its last stanza the trenchant
praise of a fellow poet. Andreini's regard for Rinuccini, however, was
deep, and her son and daughter-in-law continued the Andreini family's
collaborations with Rinuccini even after Isabella's death in 1604. An-
dreini's whereabouts during the year 1600, when *Euridice* was in pro-
duction, are not known, yet she probably encountered Rinuccini in
Florence at that time.[12] Alternatively, the two authors may have met
later in France; they certainly continued their association there, as Ri-
nuccini held a position in the retinue of Maria de' Medici from 1600 to
1604, and Andreini accepted the patronage of Henry IV from 1601 to
1604, and perhaps as early as 1599.[13]

As one might expect of a leading actress of the Renaissance stage,
Andreini had strong connections to those who wrote for the theater. Her
rapport with Rinuccini is well attested by the poems in the present vol-
ume, as is her relationship to the playwright Laura Guidiccioni Luc-
chesini. The verses Andreini penned in honor of Guidiccioni, all in
commemoration of the latter's death, speak to the close bond shared by
these two women, which is otherwise undocumented. Indeed, little is
known of the life and work of Guidiccioni. Born in Lucca in 1550, she
came to the Florentine court in 1588 and died there in 1597. Best
known for her collaborations with Emilio de' Cavalieri on various mu-
sic-theater productions, Guidiccioni composed the poetry for the final
ballo performed at the Medici wedding celebrations of 1589, which
united Francesco de' Medici and Christine of Lorraine. Known as *Il
ballo del gran duca*, this finale to the *intermedii* composed for per-
formance with Girolamo Bargagli's comedy *La pellegrina* is remark-
able in the history of music theater in that Cavalieri composed the mu-
sic first, to which Guidiccioni then adapted her poetic text.[14]

In addition to *Il ballo del gran duca*, Guidiccioni also wrote three
pastoral plays that Cavalieri set to music. All three are adaptations of
existing pastoral dramas, revised in order to accommodate a musical
setting. These pastorals, *La disperazione di Fileno* (from Giovan Do-
nato Cucchetti's *La Pazzia* of 1581), *Il satiro* (from Giovan Maria
Avanzi's *Il satiro* of 1587), and *Il giuoco della cieca* (an adaptation of
act three, scene two of Battista Guarini's *Il pastor fido* of 1589), are the
first compositions in the genre *dramma per musica*, predating Rinuc-
cini's *La Dafne* of 1598, which also does not survive, and also antici-
pating the first extant opera, Rinuccini's *Euridice* of 1600.[15]

The decade between 1588 and 1597, when both Guidiccioni and
Andreini had connections to the Florentine court, is an important one

for both women. During those years, both contributed to the wedding festivities for Francesco de' Medici and Christine of Lorraine. Andreini enacted a landmark performance of her *La pazzia d'Isabella*, which was accompanied by the *intermedii* composed for *La pellegrina* and ended with Guidiccioni's *Il ballo del gran duca*. Guidiccioni's three pastoral plays were written and performed between 1588 and 1592, during which time Andreini published her own pastoral play, *Mirtilla*.

Guidiccioni must have made a deep impression on Andreini, who was twelve years her junior, for the actress to have written the passionate works included in the present volume in her honor. The four poems—a *canzone*, two sonnets and a madrigal—comprise a delicate grouping that illuminates the stylistic variations of Andreini's lyrics and their relationships to genre and form. The *canzone* is a clear lament, incanted over the stones of Guidiccioni's tomb and serving as a Neoplatonic transcendence between earth and heaven. Its breathless stanzas speak first to the heavens, entreating pity from Guidiccioni's soul. The prayer then turns to keening, as the author pleads for death, Guidiccioni's loss signifying the loss of life itself. In the third stanza, Andreini's voice becomes that of a medium or messenger, describing the sorrow of Guidiccioni's husband. This third-person account of the grieving man gives the narrative a neoclassical aspect by removing the enactment of his grief to somewhere inaccessible to all but the enraptured poet. Finally, in a ritual re-enactment of the Orpheus myth, the entire community weeps with the bereaved husband, thus achieving the catharsis of emotion desired of all such poetry.

The sonnets Andreini writes in commemoration of Guidiccioni's death invoke a Bembist high style that displays erudition as well as emotion. "Chi pensò mai veder fra terra oscura" offers a studiously inventive imitation of Petrarch, cobbled together from the individual lines of poems from his *Rerum vulgarium fragmenta*, which paints Guidiccioni as a transformed version of Petrarch's Laura. This representation is achieved not only through the imitation of Petrarch's verses, but also (and more specifically) by way of the poem's fifth line, which speaks of Laura's transformation in the eyes of the poet. The other sonnet, "Quanti trofei già d'arme vaga, e quanti," is less academic, although its style emulates the flourishing recitation of noble battles and warriors'deeds found in epic poetry. Its lofty tone shows more pride than sorrow, in stark contrast with the weeping, distraught tenor of Andreini's madrigal on the same subject. The madrigal exhibits the intimate, masculine style typical of Andreini's compositions in this genre. Beginning with the stony, consonant-laden line "Tra questi duri sassi," the poem is an ardent outpouring that evokes its emotion through the shimmering shifts of focus that bear images of Laura, a passing traveler, the poet, and an amorphous "us."

Andreini's second book of lyric poetry (*Rime . . . parte seconda*) was printed after her death by the publishers of her first volume of *Rime*, Girolamo Bordone and Pietromartire Locarni. In comparison with the first *canzoniere*, the second volume represents a far less introspective collection that yields many more laudatory exhortations than amatory vignettes. The second book includes mainly sonnets: there are 105 of this genre, accompanied by only eighteen madrigals and a single *canzone* written by Gherardo Borgogni. Most of the poems are dedicated to a named person or academy, and many are printed with responses directed to Andreini. The publishers' preface stipulates that the volume represents the combined efforts of Andreini, her husband Francesco, and their children: "Now we make ourselves the ready executors of the will of the author, and of that of Mr. Francesco her husband, and of their children, that they desire this effect. . . ." Whereas Andreini composed the verses, Francesco probably assumed editorship of the collection, perhaps with the assistance of their eldest son Giovan Battista and his wife Virginia Ramponi Andreini.[16]

The major portion of Andreini's poems written in honor of academies and academicians appear in this second book of *Rime*, and it contains many sonnets dedicated to nobles of the French court. This volume is therefore an important source of biographical information about Andreini, since it enumerates the members of her intellectual circle and many of her patrons. In it, we find sonnets addressed to the scholars Erycius Puteanus, Antonio Maria Spelta, and Gherardo Borgogni, in company with other members of the Accademia degli Intenti of Pavia, poems in honor of various members of the Accademia Filarmonica of Verona and the Accademia Olimpica of Vicenza, and encomia to various French nobles, including Henry IV, Maria de' Medici, the Duke of Nevers, and others. This second book of *Rime* also contains poems composed by Andreini in praise of Spelta's history of Pavia, of Borgogni's verse anthology, *La fonte del diporto*, and of a history written by a Madamoiselle de Chiaramonte.[17] Andreini's *Rime . . . parte seconda* thus reflects the last three to four years of her life, after her induction into the Accademia degli Intenti in 1601, after the performance of Rinuccini's *Euridice* at the Medici court in 1600, and again in 1601, after Andreini's interaction with the Accademia Filarmonica and her journey to the French court. Andreini found a nearly inexhaustible source of patrons within the Accademia degli Intenti of Pavia. Academy members included, among a number of cardinals and other literati, Carlo Emmanuele II, the Duke of Savoy, to whom Andreini dedicated her volume of *Lettere* (posthumously published in 1607), Ranuccio Farnese, the Duke of Parma, for whom Andreini composed a sonnet on the occasion of his wedding to Margherita Aldobrandini in Rome in 1600, and Cesare II d'Este, the Duke of Ferrara and one of the Andreini family's most important patrons.[18] The academy also provided Andreini with the sponsorship of the Cardinal San Giorgio Cinzio Aldobrandini, the nephew of Pope Clement VIII and dedicatee of both of Andreini's books of *Rime*.[19]

The Accademia degli Intenti, together with several of her sister academies, further sponsored a number of the anthologies in which Andreini's verses appear. Anthologists begin to include Andreini's verses in their collections in 1587, continuing at least through 1622. Interestingly, the appearance of Andreini's poems in anthologies predates her own publications, and her inclusion in academic anthologies occurs long before she became a member of the Accademia degli Intenti in 1601. Gherardo Borgogni, a poet from Alba and a member of both the Accademia degli Intenti and the Accademia degli Inquieti, alone is responsible for at least five collections containing Andreini's verses. These are the *Gioie poetiche di madrigali*, *La fonte del diporto*, *Le muse toscane*, *Rime di diversi illustri poeti de' nostri tempi*, and *Nuova scielta di rime*.[20] Other anthologies containing Andreini's poems include *Il gareggiamento poetico*, edited by Carlo Fiamma of the Paduan Accademia degli Orditi, the *Mausoleo di poesie volgari, et latine* (1588), published in honor of Giuliano Gosellini of the Accademia degli Intenti, and the *Rime di diversi celebri poeti dell'età nostra* (1587) of Giovan Battista Licino. The five-volume collection of *canzonette* and *canzoni* by Remigio Romano, published over a period of years from 1618 to 1627, and the anthology of verses published by Pietro Cattaneo on the death of Torquato Tasso round out the poetic sources where Andreini's verses may be found. Otherwise, individual poems—principally sonnets—by Andreini occur in nonpoetic sources, such as Spelta's history of Pavia, Abate Angelo Personeni's genealogical history of Cinzio Aldobrandini's family, and Tasso's discourse in praise of marriage.[21]

Borgogni's anthologies include many poems both by and about Andreini—written by him as well as by other authors—in a series of publications dating from 1593 to 1604. Through these, he is in some part responsible for Andreini's renown as an author of lyric verse. Borgogni's own poems composed in honor of Andreini number seventeen, and she is featured in a dialogue published in his *La fonte del diporto* of 1596, reprinted in 1602.[22] In this dialogue, Borgogni talks with the fictional character Andronico, the former praising Andreini's soon-to-be-published *Rime* and offering to read the sonnet he wrote for the occasion, along with Andreini's response to it. (Borgogni's poem is entitled "Apollo, questa il cui valor," and Andreini's, "Se tu, che qui fra noi.") Andronico, who has until now known of Andreini only by reputation, pronounces her most virtuous and eloquent. This dialogue and its discussion of Andreini's *Rime* indicates that the actress' collection of lyric verse was in preparation for at least five years before its publication in 1601, and that she had a strong working relationship with at least one member of the Accademia degli Intenti before her induction in the same year.

Andreini had more tenuous connections with other academies in northern Italy, especially the Accademia Filarmonica of Verona and the Accademia Olimpica of Vicenza. The Accademia Filarmonica is Italy's oldest musical academy, and it has existed continuously since its founding in 1543.[23] The minutes of the academy from its meeting of June 22, 1601 record that one of Andreini's poems, dedicated to the *Accademici Filarmonici*, was read out to the membership. Andreini did not appear before the assemblage, and so the sonnet, "Quel ciel, che socera il liquefatto Argento," was put forward by Adriano Grandi.[24] The members judged the poem to be very beautiful and assigned Cristoforo Ferrari the task of composing a sonnet that would be sent to Andreini in response from the academy as a whole. This sonnet, "Mentre pien di stupor l'Adige intento" was read out to the membership of the Accademia Filarmonica on June 29, 1601.[25] Note the allusion at the end of the first line of Ferrari's sonnet ("l'Adige *intento*") to Andreini's membership in the Accademia degli Intenti.

Other than this single entry in the *Atti* of the Accademia Filarmonica, the only evidence we have of Andreini's relationship to the academy or its members is in the form of encomiastic sonnets printed in her second book of *Rime*.[26] Here, there are seven encomiums to Andreini by various members of the *Filarmonica* and seven responses. The sonnets are addressed to Andreini as a member of the Accademia degli Intenti, and all concentrate on the neoclassical allusions and humanistic word play that are hallmarks of Andreini's style.

Similarly, a number of sonnets printed in the *Rime . . . seconda parte* are written by members of the Accademia Olimpica of Vicenza. The Accademia Olimpica is devoted to the study and production of drama, and its glorious sixteenth-century theater still stands along the banks of the river Adige in Vicenza. The theater continues to house the original stage sets constructed for its inaugural performance of Sophocles' *Oedipus Rex* in 1585.[27] The Olympians' cast for Sophocles' tragedy included a Signora Verato (the wife of Giambattista Verato, a member of the academy) in the role of Jocasta, demonstrating that the appearance of women on the stage of the Teatro Olimpico and in the academy's performances was by no means taboo.[28] Andreini and other women clearly enjoyed freer interactions with the Accademia Olimpica and its members than they did with the Accademia Filarmonica of Verona, where women were barred from all meetings.

Andreini's sonnet "Un bel sembiante in habito negletto," written in response to Angelo Ingegneri's "In ischietto vestir vera bellezza," calls attention to one of the Accademia Olimpica's more renowned members. Ingegneri's sonnet sings of Andreini's beauty and talent, which may be discerned even when the actress is clothed in rustic dress. In her ode, Andreini picks up Ingegneri's metaphor of the beautiful figure dressed in lowly attire, but then turns it, saying that disheveled dress will cause a lovely figure to lose its grace. All this is but a metaphor for Andreini's compositional style, which Ingegneri asserts is overly contrived. The final tercet of Andreini's sonnet returns the sting of Ingegneri's so-called praise by telling him that his admiration, should he care to admire her, will not be mistaken for reproach. This pungent exchange between actress and dramatist is one of the most delightful demonstrations of the nature of Andreini's relationship with another author. The two must have known each other quite well, for Ingegneri acknowledges his debt to Andreini in the introduction to his treatise on dramatic poetry and its performance, *Della poesia rappresentativa & del modo di rappresentatre le favole sceniche*, published in 1598. He cites her pastoral play, *Mirtilla*, as one of the best theatrical compositions of the time. Ingegneri wrote the treatise, dedicated to Duke Vincenzo Gonzaga of Mantua, with the express purpose of recording contemporary theatrical practices before they vanished with the wind.[29]

La curiosa, et dilettevole aggionta, a history of the city of Pavia written by Antonio Maria Spelta in 1602, together with the great seventeenth-century history of France written by Pierre Matthieu, are important sources for documenting Andreini's relationships with various courts and academies.[30] Spelta's publication offers pride of place to a sonnet composed for the author by Andreini. Immediately following Spelta's dedication, the poem, "Molle di pianto il sen, duri lamenti," by the "Very Illustrious and Most Eloquent Isabella Andreini, Gentlewoman of Padua, Comedienne of highest rank, Member of the Accademia degli Intenti" offers praise to the name of Spelta. Spelta also includes several poems written in honor of Andreini by authors who were, like him, members of the Accademia degli Intenti, Erycius Puteanus and Filippo Massini, doctor of letters at the Studio of Pavia. He further printed several of his own verses in honor of Andreini and five poems newly composed by Andreini herself.[31]

I have included within the present volume all the poems by Andreini that were set to music and also those poems that appear in more popular anthologies than those edited by members of various literary academies. This is done to give an indication of those of Andreini's poems that transcended the scholarly sphere and gained popularity among a broader audience. The twenty poems of Andreini's that were set to music, thirteen madrigals and seven *scherzi*, were all published in her first book or *Rime*. None were reprinted in Andreini's second *canzoniere*, nor do they share concordances with the anthologies edited by Gherardo Borgogni, the Accademia degli Intenti, or Giovan Battista Licino. Two anthologies that do include some of the twenty poems are those edited by Carlo Fiamma and Remigio Romano. These two collections prove to be important, not only as sources of Andreini's lyric poetry, but of vernacular poetic texts in general at the turn of the seventeenth century.

Il gareggiamento poetico, edited by Carlo Fiamma, is a gargantuan, nine-volume collection of Italian verse, dedicated to Giulio Cesare di Capova, the Prince of Conca and habitué of the court of Naples. The text was printed under the auspices of the *Accademia degli Orditi* of Padua and includes 1,753 poems in various forms, mainly madrigals and sonnets. The collection is organized according to subject, each of the nine volumes specializing in one of the following topics: beauties, relationships, likenesses, praises, various works, mixed works, wedding pieces, playful works, and funerary madrigals. Author attributions are nearly always provided, and nearly every poem in each of the nine volumes is dedicated to some patron or honoree, many of them women.

These dedications were made by the editor of the anthology. As might be expected, there is an abundance of Anacreontic verse, as well as pastoral poetry. Andreini, favored most heavily in volume five of Fiamma's edition, is represented by thirty poems altogether: three in the first volume, six in the second, two in the third, fourteen in the fifth, three in the sixth, and one each in volumes eight and nine. These volumes include only madrigals by Andreini, two of which were later set to music: "Languisco, e son tant'anni" and "O mia Nisa, o mio cor."[32]

The five-volume anthology of *canzonette* by Remigio Romano, is an entirely different sort of collection than *Il gareggiamento poetico*. Its analysis is included here because it is primarily an anthology of poems, although its contents are intended specifically for musical performance and it includes intabulations for Spanish guitar. Thus, it is both poetic anthology and music book. Unlike *Il gareggiamento poetico*, which features mainly madrigals and sonnets, the genres in Romano's collection tend more toward the *canzonetta* and *scherzo*. Romano is not, to my knowledge, associated with any academy, and the anthology itself evinces no claims to academic affiliation. It is a set of five volumes: four *raccolte*, plus an appended *residuo* to the fourth book. Only two poems by Andreini—the *scherzi* "Io credèa che tra gli amanti" and "Deh, girate luci amate"—are included in Romano's anthology, but the number of musical settings accorded to these poems (and especially to the latter, which was set to music at least nine times) belie the importance of Romano's collection as a widely distributed and well-known source.

Romano's anthology is the only source of Andreini's poems in which lyrics are matched to preexisting musical formulas, and it is therefore the only source for which the musical settings cannot be called interpretations of their poetic texts. The publisher's introduction to the first volume tells us that the *Raccolta* is a collection of the most well-known lyrics, together with many other most beautiful and new *canzoni* that appeared in an earlier anthology edited by Romano and entitled *Sciolte*. In the second volume, the title indicates that this collection of *canzonette musicali* is "most beautiful for singing and playing on modern airs." The third volume is slightly different from the others in that it presents, not *canzonette musicali*, as in the other books, but rather "most beautiful *canzoni alla romanesca*." The fourth volume consists of *canzonette* mixed with *frottole*, and the dedication to the readers of the appended *residuo* tells us that its contents were composed by both poets and musicians. These descriptions of each volume's contents provide us with a better understanding of the likenesses and differences among poems of similar genres. The poetic contents of book three, for example, demonstrate no real difference from that of the other volumes, and we may infer that *canzoni alla romanesca* and *canzonette musicali* are, as used by Romano, synonymous terms for formulaic popular songs. The poetic genres in Romano's collection are most often *scherzi* in the style of Chiabrera, although other sorts of lyric texts also appear. Each book of the anthology is organized alphabetically according to the first lines of the poems.

The musical accompaniments in Romano's anthology consist of Spanish guitar intabulations added to some of the verses. Only 43 of the 454 texts, however, are printed with intabulations, although the other poems are to be set as well, according to the performer's judgment and with the assistance of other musical instructions accompanying many of the poems. Andreini's texts are not printed with intabulations, although her *scherzo* "Io credèa che tra gli amanti," appears in volume one with an instruction to sing the published text to the tune of a popular song: "a most beautiful air on the one that begins, 'Caro labbro vermiglietto.'" Unfortunately, no musical setting of "Caro labbro vermiglietto" is known to survive.

We may conclude from the ordering of Romano's collection—within each volume, alphabetically, according to first lines—and from the sporadic inclusion of guitar intabulations, that the primary purpose of the publication was to assist performers in remembering the words of popular poems. Secondarily, the collection might serve as a guide to adapting new verses to existing songs. The first lines of the poetic texts must have been as familiar to the musicians who used Romano's anthology as the accompaniments to which they would be sung, for if the first line of a text is not known, there is no way of finding it within the organizational scheme of the collection without reading through its entire contents. Similarly, guitar intabulations are identified only by the texts they accompany and are not given titles such as "La Spagna," "Canzona di Firenze" or "Lamento d'Arianna." Neither are the poems grouped by either genre or subject, classifications that would make it possible to locate texts by type rather than by their first lines. Romano's publication must therefore be seen as a reference book for the experienced performer rather than a source which could be used without extensive prior knowledge of the repertory. In this, it is analogous to the published scenarios of *commedia dell'arte* companies, and similar methodologies may be developed for assessing both types of sources, based on performers' intermixing of improvisation with preexisting written material in the creation of the musical or theatrical work.

Romano's collection highlights the cultural significance of Andreini's *scherzo* "Deh, girate, luci amate" by including a parody of it by an unknown author. This anonymous competitive poem, "Deh, mirate, luci ingrate," appears in volume one of the collection. Andreini's poem, printed in volume two, and the anonymous *scherzo* "compete" in terms of their opening lines, meter, rhyme scheme and the subject of eyes. The anonymous poem consists of only four strophes, as follows:

Deh, mirate
Luci ingrate
Il dolor de la partita.
Mio partire
È morire,
Occhi belli aita, aita.

Ahi sdegnose,
Ahi ritrose,
Voi sprezzate il suon de' carmi?
Lui fere,
Luci altere
Voi gridate a l'armi, a l'armi.

Fero ardore
Strugge il core,
Chi vien meno a poco a poco?
Chi m'accende
Non m'intende,
E pur grido al foco, al foco.

Cor ferito
Cor tradito
Fuggi meco hormai partiamo?
Tua mercede
Non ha fede;
Non tardar, andiamo, andiamo.

Andreini's Anacreontic *scherzo* speaks of the joys of love, likening the eyes of the beloved to sweet darts that are more ardent than the sun and dwelling on her vermillion mouth, which separates the lover's heart from his breast. In contrast, "Deh, mirate luci ingrate" talks of disdain and the torment inflicted on a lover by the beloved's eyes when his ardor is not returned. By the final strophe, the lover asks, "will you flee with me at last? Your mercy is faithless, but do not tarry, let's go, let's go." Although the meter and rhyme scheme of the poems are identical, enabling them to be set to the same musical accompaniment, the poems' styles are quite different. The author of the second poem delights in repeating words to round off each strophe, lending a strong sense of closure to each stanza. All four stanzas are otherwise divided by a full stop at the end of line three, whereas Andreini's poem tends to elide the first and second systems of each strophe, working against the structural division imposed by the longer, eight-syllable meter of lines three and six. The anonymous author employs more examples of anaphora—the repetition of a word or words at the beginnings of lines or stanzas. Andreini's text, in contrast, evinces a more subtle use of structural elements, employing consonant and vowel sounds to suggest anaphora, as in stanzas three and four, where the words "Dolce" and "Da," "Più" and "Pio," and "Che" and "Cara" are allied using this technique. Andreini's text also demonstrates a different, more wholistic approach to syntax, emphasizing the comprehensive meaning of the poem rather than that of individual strophes.

Rhetorical devices proper to the oral recitation of poetry, such as anaphora, asyndeton, metaphor, and repetition, may be found in much of Andreini's poetry. The *scherzo* "Io credèa che tra gli amanti" offers some good examples. In this multistrophe Petrarchan poem, each of the first four stanzas begins with the same words: "Io credèa . . . ," meaning, "I thought . . . ." The anaphoric device functions almost as a refrain, reinforcing in the listeners' ears the central conceit of the poem. In the *Ars rhetorica*, Aristotle condones various kinds of repetition within spoken oratory, but says they are inappropriate to the written word: "frequent repetition of the same word [is] rightly disapproved in written speech, but in public debate even rhetoricians make use of [it]."[33] Later, in stanzas five and six of Andreini's *scherzo*, the image of thinking is invoked again in the phrases "non pensai" and "Nè credèa," although the opening flourish, "Io credèa . . . " has been abandoned. Throughout the text of the *scherzo*, the speaker expresses disbelief in the effects of love. No matter how hard he thinks about and tries to rationalize the vicissitudes and sorrows of love, finally he must succomb to its yearnings.

In the same poem, the rhetorician's asyndeton, or the omission of conjunctions, is employed, it seems, to give emphasis. This, too, is a device encouraged by Aristotle in spoken rhetoric and discouraged in written works.[34] Its use in the first stanza, together with the repetition of the word "sol" or "solo," amplfies the sorrow felt by the poem's subject, as he identifies himself with all lovers.

The prevalence of rhetorical gestures is in part dependent on the form of the poem in which they are used. Madrigals allow more verse space for the development of metaphors, and the short lines in *scherzi* encourage the use of asyndeta. Repetition, anaphora, and asyndeton are less prevalent in Andreini's madrigals than they are in her *scherzi*, whereas the madrigals make far greater use of imagistic metaphor. In her *scherzi*, the strophic form and regular alternation of four- and eight-syllable lines fosters text repetition, anaphora, and asyndeton, and most of her poems in this form use some of each.

Repetition, anaphora, and asyndeton often occur together at the beginning of *scherzo* stanzas. The pairing of the opening lines by means of parallel rhetorical statements is a specific trademark of Chiabrera's *scherzi*, and Andreini often employs this device in her own. Chiabrera's intensive infusion of the technique may be seen in "Dolci miei sospiri."[35]

> *Dolci miei sospiri,*
> *Dolci miei martiri,*
> *Dolce mio desio,*
> *E voi dolci canti,*
> *E voi dolci pianti:*
> *Rimanete, a Dio.*

The second strophe of Andreini's "Care gioie, che le noie" demonstrates her use of the idiom, in which single repetition and repetitions of consonant sounds are typical.

> *Hor non finge,*
> *Hor non pinge*
> *Con sua squadra falsa, e vaga*
> *Sogno vano*
> *Quella mano,*
> *Che si dolce il sen m'impiaga.*

Chiabrera and Andreini both use anaphora in a manner different than the anonymous author of "Deh, mirate luci ingrate." The author of that poem uses paired repeated words at the beginning of the first two lines, again in the fourth and fifth lines, and at the beginning of the third and sixth lines. In this case, all lines that rhyme also begin with the same word. The author accentuates the repetitive style of the poem by echoing the end of the last phrase of the stanza, "a l'armi, a l'armi." In this poem, the result of these repetitions is a structural rigor in each double-system stanza that, while interesting and inventive in itself, detracts from the large-scale form:

Ahi sedgnose,
Ahi ritrose,
Voi sprezzate il suon de' carmi?
Luci fere,
Luci altere
Voi gridate a l'armi, a l'armi.

Andreini's madrigals, in contrast, are through-composed poems featuring freely alternating seven- and eleven-syllable lines and a variable rhyme scheme. This organizational liberty enables the poet to interpret most effectively the meaning of the verse. The number of lines per stanza varies from poem to poem. Each madrigal, however, usually provides for a concluding couplet within its verse structure, which is set off from the rest of the stanza by some combination of meter, rhyme and syntax. Examples of the kinds of formal variation present in Andreini's madrigal style may be seen in three texts: "Amorosa mia Clori," "O mia Nisa, o mio cor," and "Quella bocca di rose."

The first of these, "Amorosa mia Clori," offers a good example of a structurally coherent madrigal text in which meter, rhyme, and syntax work together to produce a clearly balanced, unified whole. In this poem, meter and syntax are closely related. There is no enjambment between lines, and the structural pauses in the syntax correspond, in all but one instance, with the metric scheme. Thus, the metric organization of the strophe (the alternation of seven- and eleven-syllable lines) follows a pattern of 3+3+2+2, and the syntactical structure shows the pattern 3+2+(1+2)+2. At those points where the two structural levels intersect, specifically at the ends of lines three, six, and eight, the internal cadences are strongest. Where the metrical and syntactical nodes do not correspond, as at the end of line five, the syntactically strong cadence created by the completion of the sentence is suspended. By introducing the rhyme pattern into this formal construct, we find that the sequence 4+4+2 further strengthens the caesura at the end of line eight, but that it detracts from prior cadences by conflicting with the metrical and syntactical schemes.

Organizational stability is most useful at the beginnings and ending of madrigal stanzas, because it provides a sense of introduction and then closure. In the middle lines, however, structural ambiguity, due to the suspension or abeyance of strong cadence points, offers a sense of forward motion and, ultimately, formal coherence. These functions of stability and ambiguity are equally relevant to poetic and musical composition, and are two of the primary factors in determining the efficacy of a composer's approach to text setting.

The formal organization of "O mia Nisa, o mio cor" differs from that of "Amorosa mia Clori," yet it offers an equally strong structure. The meter and syntax, which follow an overall pattern of 4+2, are closely allied in contrast to the poem's rhyme scheme. The metric configuration offers a fairly strong internal cadence at the end of line four. The syntax, however, provides a strong pattern of (3+1)+2, which reinforces the break after line four, adding to the momentum of the opening quatrain and strengthening the integrity of the final couplet. In contrast, the rhyme scheme emphasizes a symmetrical pattern of 3+3, thereby undermining the impact of the closing couplet.

The third example, "Quella bocca di rose," demonstrates a more refined sense of formal organization. Here, the meter provides strong structural anchors at the ends of lines five and eight, in a pattern that is generally deemphasized in the stanza's rhyme scheme. The syntax, most closely allied to the meter of the stanza, provides a full stop in the middle of line five, but the aside, "(Ahi, scaltra Pastorella!)," enables a change of subject and the beginning of a new structural segment with the interjection, "Ecco," in line six. There is no enjambment at the end of line five to obscure the metric cadence. Both meter and syntax offer a weak cadence at the end of line two, although a pause is created by a syntactical inversion. The rhyme scheme reinforces the idea of a closing couplet, but the meter and syntax so strongly override the cadence at the end of line six that an insistence on the convention of a concluding couplet, as opposed to a final terzet, would need to rely as much on the generic structural paradigm as on the specific formal organization of the stanza.

We have seen in the examples "Amorosa mia Clori," "O mia Nisa, o mio cor," and "Quella bocca di rose" a sampling of the structural types present in Andreini's madrigals. While in general these poems adhere to standard madrigalian practices of the late sixteenth century, the author's responses to questions of organization and form vary from the straightforward and clear organizational patterns evinced in "Amorosa mia Clori" and "O mia Nisa, o mio cor," to the subtler ambiguities of "Quella bocca di rose." In all of Andreini's madrigals, the formal structure of the stanza generally works to reinforce the syntax and affect of the poem.

As is true of the madrigal genre as a whole, Andreini's madrigals are through composed and each is devoted to the explication of a single affect, situation, or metaphor. Some conclude in an epigrammatic punch line, as in "Languisco, e son tant'anni" and "O bellissimo petto," and most indulge in vivid Petrarchan imagery, as do "Doppo la pioggia del mio pianto amaro" and "Per lo soverchio affanno."

In "Languisco, e son tant'anni," syntax and rhyme scheme reinforce the poem's affective style and epigrammatic character. The first two lines concentrate on the poem's subject: *I* languish. Beginning with the enjambment at the end of line two which joins "e voi" with "Non date fede," the meaning is focused on Tigre, the object of the affections expressed in the stanza: *You* will believe me, *you* will have pity on my fate. The closing couplet offers the moral to this miniature tale of love and death: pity is too late if it arrives after the death of the lover who may die for want of it. This Petrarchan theme is recalled and parodied in the tale-type of a shepherd who attempts suicide because of unrequited love, as Igilio does in his anguish for the nymph Fillide, and Tirsi for Mirtilla, in Andreini's pastoral play, *Mirtilla*.

"O bellissimo petto" embodies a similar pithy style, couched in grand melancholic sentiment. Again, as in "Languisco, e con tant'anni," this is an eight-line stanza divided into sections of 3+3+2 by the meter, rhyme scheme, and syntax. The focus of the stanza remains concentrated for the first six lines on the beloved's breast. The final couplet, further accentuated by the interjection, "No, no," signals a change of heart in the poem's subject, and offers an epigrammatic reversal of the sentiment expressed in the first six lines.

Much of Andreini's poetry favors a Petrarchan style of contrasts, melancholy, and imagery. In "Doppo la pioggia del mio pianto amaro," the langorous sorrow of unrequited love is transformed into a visual aspect of beauty, to be cherished as an ideal state of love. In this madrigal, the vivid visual images of rain showers and sunlight, which make rainbows in nature, are translated into showers of tears and the light that streams from a beloved's eyes. The resulting rainbow causes the spurned lover's face to be bathed in iridescence. The beautiful, prismatic illumination remains only as long as the subject of the poem sheds tears of sorrow, and thus the lover's pain is evidence of something beautiful and precious. The rhetorial stance of the poem is embodied in Andreini's use of a visual metaphor, one of the types of metaphor recommended by Aristotle: "Metaphors therefore should be derived from what is beautiful either in sound, or in signification, or to sight, or to some other sense."[36]

"Per lo soverchio affanno" also expresses melancholy through metaphor, wrought from the sorrows of a lover's rejection. Here, the familiar juxtaposition of ardent flames and cold ice signal the lover's despair as he approaches death, eyes closed and complexion pale. Opportunities for affective musical setting occur throughout the stanza, on words like "spirti dolenti," "fiamma ardenti," "freddo ghiaccio," "chiudo le luci," "mi scoloro," and "io moro," which are often depicted musically with chromatic harmonies, alternately rapid or slow rhythms, rests and changes in meter, harmonic rhythm and texture. The poetic style thus encourages an affective musical setting without demanding a direct, personal interpretation of a single lover's torments. The sentiments evoked in "Per lo soverchio affanno," as in Andreini's other madrigals, are universal expressions of a stylized Petrarchan aesthetic of love.

The last group of sonnets in the collection (exchanges with Ottavio Rinuccini, Cosimo Ruggieri, Archangelo Zuccaro, and Agostin Gioioso da Sanseverino) show Andreini at a new game. She is writing in response to other poets, and in so doing adopts their form, subject matter, allusions, and rhyme scheme. Indeed, in all but one of the exchanges, Andreini matches the other poet's rhyming words, letter for letter, as she seeks to temper his praise of her talents and beauty. These sonnets were written at the court of France in the very first years of the seventeenth century, and they seem clearly to be the results of a parlor game. Ottavio Rinuccini begins the game, with a sonnet in praise of Cornelia Doni Gorini. In the final tercet, he invites Andreini to add her praises to his, calling for the actress to tune up her lyre ("Tempro la cetra"). Andreini, perhaps getting used to the game, adopts Rinuccini's rhymes—but not the exact words of his rhymes—and stumbles a bit through the sonnet until she proclaims her hopes of being able to sing Gorini's praises in the future. She warms quickly to the game's subtleties, though, and in response to Cosimo Ruggiero's fulsome admiration of her poetic flair, writes that she will hope for a place in heaven by following his wise example. Archangelo Zuccaro steps up next with an ode to Andreini's pen that demands of her an opening line ending in "chisel." She rises to Zuccaro's challenge, declaring her chisel to have grown dull, and proudly states that Father Time would have to cut the tongue from her head in order to stop her writing poetry. By the end of the sonnet, however, Andreini renounces Zuccaro's prophecy that she will be the immortal poet of the age and places him, instead, on the throne of glory. Finally, Agostin Gioioso da Sanseverino pens a lovely poem in honor of Andreini's dramatic gifts, which the actress gracefully turns into a paean to his own dulcet song.

Notes

1. The entire surviving correspondence between Andreini and Puteanus is transcribed and translated in my *Music and Women of the Commedia dell'Arte* (Oxford: Oxford University Press, 2003), 305-23.
2. See Frank J. Warnke, "Gaspara Stampa: Aphrodite's Priestess, Love's Martyr," in *Women Writers of the Renaissance and Reformation*, ed. Katharina M. Wilson (Athens: University of Georgia Press, 1987), 3-21; Joseph Gibaldi, "Vittoria Colonna: Child, Woman, and Poet," in ibid., 22-46; Richard Poss, "Veronica Gambara: A Renaissance Gentildonna," in ibid., 47-57; Frank J. Warnke, *Three Women Poets: Renaissance and Baroque: Louise Labé, Gaspara Stampa, and Sor Juana Inés de la Cruz* (Lewisburg, PA: Bucknell University Press, 1987); Margaret F. Rosenthal, *The Honest Courtesan: Veronica Franco, Citizen and Writer in Sixteenth-Century Venice* (Chicago: University of Chicago Press, 1992), 155; *Gaspara Stampa: Selected Poems*, ed. and trans. Laura Anna Stortoni and Mary Prentice Lillie (New York: Italica Press, 1994).
3. Cinzio Aldobrandini is known as Cardinal San Giorgio, San Giorgio being the name of his titular church. This designation helps to distinguish him from his cousin, Pietro Aldobrandini, who is known as Cardinal Aldobrandini. Both cardinals served jointly as secretary of state to their uncle, Pope Clement VIII.

4. See Luigi Baldacci, *Il petrarchismo italiano nel cinquecento* (Padua: s.n., 1974), and Ferdinando Taviani, "Bella d'Asia: Torquato Tasso, gli attori e l'immortalità," *Paragone/letteratura* 35 (1984): 3-76.

5. See Donna Cardamone, *The canzona villanesca alla napolitana and Related Forms, 1537-1570)* (Ann Arbor: UMI Research Press, 1981), 92, and Gary Tomlinson, *Monteverdi and the End of the Renaissance* (Berkeley: University of California Press, 1987), 210-14.

6. Gabriello Chiabrera, *Canzonette, rime varie, dialoghi di Gabriello Chiabrera*, ed. Luigi Negri (Turin: Unione, 1964), 564, as cited in Paolo Fabbri, *Monteverdi*, trans. Tim Carter (Cambridge, UK: Cambridge University Press), 73.

7. See Pierre de Ronsard, *Les Quatre prémiers livres des Odes de Pierre de Ronsard* (Paris: G. Cavellat, 1550); Laura Jeanice Brooks, "French Chanson Collections on the Texts of Pierre de Ronsard, 1570-1580," 2 vols. (Ph.D. dissertation: The Catholic University of America, 1990); Margaret McGowan, *Ideal Forms in the Age of Ronsard* (Berkeley: University of California Press, 1985).

8. See Ferdinando Neri, *Il Chiabrera e la Pleiade francese* (Turin: Fratelli Bocca, 1920); Gabriello Chiabera, *Scherzi e canzonette morali di Gabriello Chiabrera* (Genoa: Giuseppe Pavoni, 1599); idem, *Le maniere de' versi toscani* (Genoa: Giuseppe Pavoni, 1599).

9. Other of Andreini's *scherzi* are also dedicated to Chiabrera, although only in the later editions of her first book of *Rime*. These include "Io credèa che tra gli amanti" and "Movèa dolce un zefiretto." The printer may have added these dedications after Andreini's death as a publishing ploy, in order to increase interest in the volume, or he may have printed them in response to the wishes of the author, expressed before she died.

10. Further information on all the musical composers and musical genres mentioned in this introduction may be found in Anne MacNeil, *Music and the Life and Work of Isabella Andreini: Humanistic Attitudes toward Music, Poetry, and Theater during the Late Sixteenth and Early Seventeenth Centuries* (PhD dissertation: University of Chicago, 1994) and in the *New Grove Dictionary of Music and Musicians*, 2nd ed., ed. Stanley Sadie (London: Macmillan, 2001).

11. Andreini's daughter-in-law, Virginia Ramponi Andreini, sang the role of Arianna at the Mantuan wedding of 1608, and she is known to have worked with Rinuccini on several other occasions. Maria Stampino (University of Miami) is currently preparing a book on Rinuccini's poetry and his contributions to Renaissance music theater.

12. The Comitato Nazionale per le Celebrazioni del Quarto Centenario della Nascita dell'Opera, together with the Ministero per i Beni e le Attività Culturali, sponsored a new production of Rinuccini's *Euridice* on the exact date of its four-hundredth anniversary, October 6, 2000, in the Sala Bianca of the Palazzo Pitti in Florence, where the opera had its first performance. It is intriguing to consider the possibility that Andreini may have been among the honored guests on the original occasion.

13. The wedding celebration of Henry IV and Maria de' Medici is described in some detail by Angelo Solerti in *Musica, ballo e drammatica alla corte medicea dal 1600 al 1637* (New York: Benjamin Blom, 1968). Chiabrera also attended the festivities; see Nino Pirrotta, "Monteverdi's Poetic Choices," in *Music and Culture in Italy from the Middle Ages to the Baroque* (Cambridge, MA: Harvard University Press, 1984), 292, and Massimo Ossi, "Claudio Monteverdi's *Ordine novo, bello et gustevole*: the Canzonetta as Dramatic Module and Formal Archetype," *Journal of the Amercan Musicological Society* 45 (1992): 261-304. For the most recent chronology of Andreini's travels, see my *Music and Women of the Commedia dell'Arte*, 187-264.

14. Scolarly literature on the Medici wedding celebrations of 1589 is vast. For a good overview, see James Saslow, *The Medici Wedding of 1589: Florentine Festival as* Theatrum mundi (New Haven, CT: Yale University Press, 1996). For Andreini's and Guidiccioni's contributions to the festivities, see Anne MacNeil, "The Divine Madness of Isabella Andreini," *Journal of the Royal Musical Association* 120 (1995): 195-215; Warren Kirkendale, *L'Aria di Fiorenza, id est Il ballo del gran duca* (Florence: Leo S. Olschki, 1972).

15. See Warren Kirkendale, "L'Opera in musica prima del Peri: Le pastorali perdute di Laura Guidiccioni ed Emilio de' Cavalieri," in *Musica e spettacolo: Scienze dell'uomo e della natura*, vol. 2 of *Firenze e la Toscana dei Medici nell'Europa del '500* (Florence: Leo S. Olschki, 1983).

16. After Giovan Battista, five of Isabella and Francesco Andreini's children are known. Of the sons, Pietro Paolo was a Vallambrosian monk living near Milan and Domenico entered the military service of the Duke of Mantua. The three daughters all took the veil, although the eldest, Lavinia, spent two years in the court of Eleonora de' Medici Gonzaga before entering a convent in Mantua. Giovan Battista was the only child to adopt his parents' profession in the commedia dell'arte.

17. In 1994, I wrote that I was unable to locate any history written by a female author under the name Chiaramonte, de Chiaramonte, Claire-

monte or du Clairemonte or de Clermont. This lacuna has since been remedied, but because I have not yet had occasion to make a systematic study of the manuscript, I will not undertake discussion of it here.

18. Other noteworthy members of the Accademia degli Intenti include Antonio Maria Spelta, Gherardo Borgogni, Erycius Puteanus, and Justus Lipsius. Andreini is the only known female member of the academy. Often confused with the Accademia degli Intenti of Milan, the Pavian group was founded in 1593, in emulation of its sister organization, the Accademia degli Affidati. The two academies are closely linked from that time on. The Intenti's founders were Carlo Bossi and Celso Adorno, and its center of activity was the College of Canevanova. The avowed purpose of the academy was to publish works on all the liberal sciences and to conduct a Lyceum and School of Letters and Public Professions. The academy was dedicated to the arts of poetry, oratory and every other sort of erudition, together with the art of music. See Michele Maylender, *Storia delle accademie d'Italia* (Bologna: Licinio Cappelli, 1927), 320. In order not to interfere with classes at the university, the academy held its lectures on Sundays.

19. Andreini herself dedicated the first book of *Rime* to Cinzio Aldobrandini, while the second book was dedicated to him by the publishers Girolamo Bordone and Pietromartire Locarni.

20. Gherardo Borgogni, ed. *La fonte del diporto, dialogo del Sig. Gherardo Borgogni, d'Alba Pompea, L'Errante academico inquieto di Milano* (Venice: Giovan Battista Ciotti, 1602); idem, *Gioie poetiche di madrigali del Sig. Hieronimo Casone, e d'altri celebri poeti de' nostri tempi* (Pavia: Heredi di Bartoli, 1593); idem, *Le muse toscane di diversi nobilissimi ingegni* (Bergamo: Comin Ventura, 1594); idem, *Nuova scielta di rime* (Bergamo: Comino Ventura, 1592); idem, *Raccolta di diversi autori* (Bergamo: Comino Ventura, 1594); idem, *Rime di diversi illustri poeti de' nostri tempi* (Venice: La Minima Compagnia, 1599).

21. Giovan Battista Licino, ed., *Rime di diversi celebri poeti dell'età nostra* (Bergamo: Comino Ventura, 1587); Carlo Fiamma, *Il gareggiamento poetico del Confuso accademico ordito*, 9 vols. (Venice: Barezzo Barezzi, [1611]); Remigio Romano, *Prima raccolta di bellissime canzonette musicali, e moderne, di autori gravissimi nella poesia, & nella musica* (Vicenza: Angelo Salvadori, 1618, 1622); *Seconda raccolta di canzonette musicali; bellissime per cantare & sonare, sopra arie moderne* (Vicenza: Angelo Salvadori, 1620); *Terza raccolta di bellissime canzoni alla romanesca. Per suonare, e cantare*

nella chitara alla Spagnuola, con la sua intavolatura. Con altre
canzonette vaghe, & belle (Vicenza: Angelo Salvadori, 1620, 1622);
*Nuova raccolta di bellissime canzonette musicali, e moderne, di auttori
gravissimi nella poesia, & nella musica* (Venice: Angelo Salvadori,
1623, 1625); *Ressiduo alla quarta parte di canzonette musicali. Di
auttori gravissimi nella poesia et nella musica* (Venice: Angelo
Salvadori, 1626); Angelo Personeni, *Notizie genealogiche storiche
critiche e letterarie del Cardinale Cinzio Personeni da Ca Passero
Aldobrandini nipote di Clemente VIII* (Bergamo: Francesco Locatelli,
1786); Torquato Tasso, *Discorso in lode del matrimonio ed un dialogo
d'amore del Sig. Torquato Tasso* (Milan: Tini, 1586).

22. Borgogni, *La fonte del diporto*, 150-53; Vittorio Amedio Arullani,
*Di Gherardo Borgogni letterato albese e delle relazioni di lui con
alcuni poeti suoi contemporanei: Tommaso Stigliani, Isabella Andreini,
Torquato Tasso* (Alba: Sansoldi, 1910), 9-16.

23. *Atti e memorie della Accademia,* ed. Accademia di Agricoltura,
Scienze e Lettere di Verona (Verona: La Tipografica Veronese, 1941);
Carlo Bologna, Gian Paolo Marchi, and Enrico Paganuzzi,
*L'Accademia Filarmonica di Verona per il bicentenario mozartiano
(1791-1991)* (Verona: Accademia Filarmonica di Verona, 1991).

24. During the course of my research, I have been reassured most ve-
hemently by the archivist of the Archivio dell'Accademia Filarmonica
di Verona and current member of the academy, Enrico Paganuzzi, that
women were *never* allowed in the academy. Ellen Rosand has dis-
cussed the general reluctance to admit women in Italian academies in
her article, "Barbara Strozzi, *virtuosissima cantatrice*: The Composer's
Voice," *Journal of the American Musicological Society* 31 (1978): 241-
81.

25. Archivio dell'Accademia Filarmonica di Verona, registro 41: Atti
1601-1605, fols. 53v-56r.

26. It must be noted that the academy's records for the years 1576-1601
do not survive. See Anthony Newcomb, *The Madrigal at Ferrara
1579-1597*, 2 vols. (Princeton, NJ: Princeton University Press, 1980), I:
87.

27. The secondary literature on the Accademia Olimpica and its per-
formance of *Oedipus Rex* is extensive. For an overview and general
bibliography, see Franco Mancini, Maria Teresa Muraro and Elena
Povoledo, *I teatri del Veneto: Verona, Vicenza, Belluno, e il loro
territorio*, 3 vols. (Venice: Corbo e Fiore, 1985), II: 197-233.

28. Fernando Rigon, *Il Teatro Olimpico a Vicenza* (Milan: Electa, 1989), 48.

29. Angelo Ingegneri, *Della poesia rappresentativa & del modo di rappresentar le favole sceniche* (Ferrara: Vittorio Baldini, 1598); ed. Maria Luisa Doglio (Ferrara: Edizioni Panini, 1989).

30. Spelta, *La curiosa, et dilettevole aggionta del Sig. Ant. Maria Spelta, cittadino pavese, all'historia sua; nella quale oltra la vaghezza di molte cose, che dall'anno 1596 fino al 1603 s'intendono, sono anco omponimenti arguit, da quali non poco gusto gli elevati spiriti potranno prendere* (Pavia: Pietro Bartoli, 1602); Pierre Matthieu, *Histoire de France, et des choses memorables, advenues aux provinces estrangeres durant sept annes de paix. Du regne du Roy Henry IIII, Roy de France & de Navarre. Divisee en sept livres* (Paris: Chez I. Metayer imprimeur du Roy, & M. Guillemot, 1606).

31. Puteanus's Latin poem, "Quisquis es, Quam vides, & quam audis Venerare," appears also in the 1605 printing of Andreini's *Rime* (Milan: Girolamo Bordone and Pietromartire Locarni, 1605); Massini's sonnet, "Vesta, o Coturno altero, o socco humile," is accompanied in Spelta's text by a response from Andreini entitled "Più non tem'io gli ingiuriosi danni"; Spelta's Latin encomium, "O Quam te memorem, quoteiam nomine segnem," was written the morning after he saw Andreini perform in a pastoral play (see Spelta, *La curiosa, et dilettevole aggionta*, 169). After Andreini was called to France by Henry IV, she and her company stopped briefly in Turin and Andreini composed the sonnets, "Girando al fin le amiche sfere intorno" for Carlo Emanuele, the Duke of Savoy, "Quando a gli Dei superbi Tempi alzaro" for Donna Matilda of Savoy, "E' danza, o pugna questa? Ecco, s'io miro" on the occasion of a court ball, during which the cavaliers abducted the ladies, and "Ridean gli antri, e le Valli, e le campagne" for Don Amedeo of Savoy.

32. Andreini's poems are disposed as follows: vol. 1: "Vezzosa pargoletta," "Mano vera cagion," "Standomi a piè"; vol. 2: "Tosto, ch'a voi," "Io vi prego," "Tu m'uccidesti," "Custode invidioso," "Vide Lesbin Nisida," "Porta la Donna mia"; vol. 3: "Generoso destriero," "Tu che vai riguardando"; vol. 5: "M'è si caro il languire," "Se non è cosa in terra," "Perche più grave sia," "Timida lingua alhor," "Ahi qual mi serpe," "Morte uccider volea," "Da te m'allontanai," Se quanto bella siete," "Se da colei, che morte," "Languisco, e son tant'anni," "Pur vede nel mio volto," "Qualhor candida," "Cerca Venere il figlio," "Gia l'alma ti donai"; vol. 6: "Quest'empia donna," "Chiudami gli occhi,"

"O mia Nisa, o mio cor"; vol. 8: "Se per tuo albergo Amore"; vol. 9: Tra questi duri sassi."

33. Aristotle, *The "Art" of Rhetoric*, trans. John Henry Freese (Cambridge, MA: Harvard University Press, 1991), 419.

34. Ibid., 421.

35. This seven-strophe text is set to music by Claudio Monteverdi and published in his *Scherzi musicali* of 1607.

36. Aristotle, *The "Art" of Rhetoric*, 358-59.

Chapter 2
Selections from
Rime d'Isabella Andreini Padovana, comica gelosa
(1601)

Sonetto Primo

S'Alcun sia mai, che i versi miei negletti
Legga, non creda à questi finti ardori,
Che ne le Scene imaginati amori
Usa à trattar con non leali affetti: 4

Con bugiardi non men con finti detti
De le Muse spiegai gli alti furori:
Talhor piangendo i falsi miei dolori,
Talhor cantando i falsi miei diletti;   8

E come ne' Teatri hor Donna, ed hora
Huom fei rappresentando in vario stile
Quanto volle insegnar Natura, ed Arte.   11

Così la stella mia seguendo ancora
Di fuggitiva età nel verde Aprile
Vergai con vario stil ben mille carte.   14

Sonnet 1

If ever there is anyone who reads
These my neglected poems, don't believe
In their feigned ardors; loves imagined in
Their scenes I've handled with emotions false: 4

The Muses' inspirations high I have
Set forth with lies—no less with weasel words—
When my false sorrows sometimes I bewail,
Or sometimes sing my spurious delights;   8

And, as in theaters, in varied style,
I now have played a woman, now a man,
As Nature would instruct and Art as well,   11

So in green April, following once more
My star of fleeting years, with varied style
I ruled lines for at least a thousand leaves.   14

Sonetto IV

Qual Ruscello veggiam d'acque sovente
Povero scaturir d'alpestre vena
Sì, che temprar pon le sue stille à pena
Di stanco Peregrin la sete ardente   4

Ricco di pioggia poi farsi repente
Superbo sì, che nulla il corso affrena
Di lui, che'mperioso il tutto mena
Ampio tributo à l'Ocean possente;   8

Tal da principio havea debil possanza
A danno mio questo tiranno Amore,
E chiese in van de' miei pensier la palma.   11

Hora sovra'l mio cor tanto s'avanza,
Che rapido ne porta il suo furore
A morte il Senso, e la Ragione, e l'Alma.   14

Sonnet 4

How often do we see a little stream
That trickles from Alpine springs so meagerly
Its scanty drops can scarcely slake at all
A weary pilgrim's parched and burning thirst,   4

Enriched with rain, grow suddenly so proud
That nothing can restrain it in its course,
For, grown imperious, it carries all
In ample tribute to the mighty sea;   8

Likewise, at first, this tyrant love had but
A weak ability to do me harm
And begged in vain for victory o'er my thoughts.   11

But now, he overmasters so my heart
That speedily his furor drives to death
My Feelings, and my Reason, and my Soul.   14

Sonetto V

Spirando l'aure placide, e seconde
Al lampeggiar di due luci serene
La nave del desio carca di spene
Sciolse'l mio cor dal'amorose sponde;   4

Quando'l raggio benigno ecco s'asconde,
E spumoso fremendo il Mar diviene,
Ed hor al Cielo, hor à le nere arene
Del profondo sentier ne portan l'onde;   8

Cresce la tempestosa empia procella;
Tal che la tema è viè maggior de l'arte,
E vince ogni saper Fortuna avversa.   11

Così trà duri scogli in ogni parte
Spezzata la mia debil Navicella
Ne gli Abissi del duol cadde sommersa.   14

Sonnet 5

When placid breezes breathe, and when two lamps
Are lit and cast their glow, my heart can steer
Desire's ship, laden with my hope, away
From amorous coasts and from the shoals of love.   4

With that benign ray clouded over, lo,
The sea becomes a raging froth of spume,
And now to the sky, now to the gloomy deep's
Abyssal wastes, the waves are tossing it;   8

The wicked storm grows more tempestuous,
So that one's fear grows greater than one's skill,
And then ill Fortune conquers all one knows.   11

Thus midst dangerous shoals on every side
My fragile little barque is broken up
And sinks, submerged in sorrow's deep abyss.   14

Sonetto IX

O Non men crudo, e rio, che bello, e vago
Pur à tua voglia tu mi leghi e snodi;
E pur con mille inusitati modi
M'affligi, e del mio pianto ancor se' vago.   4

Quando sarai del sospirar mio pago?
Quando avverrà, che del mio mal non godi?
Crudel tu fuggi, e'l mio pregar non odi,
Cruda Tigre son forse, ò fiero Drago?   8

Volgiti, ascolta, arresta il passo un poco;
Accogli ingrato i lagrimosi preghi,
Vedi come per te tutta mi sfaccio.   11

Questa sola mercè non mi si nieghi,
S'arder meco non vuoi dentr'al mio foco
Deh m'insegna à gelar dentr'al tuo ghiaccio.   14

Sonnet 9

O no less wicked, cruel, than charming, fair,
Still to your will, you bind me—and unbind;
And still with a thousand new vexations you
Distress me, and are unmoved by my tears.   4

When will you have due payment from my sighs?
When come a time you won't enjoy my pain?
Cruel one, you flee, and do not hear my prayer;
Am I perhaps a tiger wild or dragon fierce?   8

Turn back and listen, slow your pace a bit;
Accept, ungrateful one, my tearful prayers;
See how, for you, I'm utterly undone.   11

This grace alone do not deny me please:
If you won't burn within my fire with me,
Ah, teach me how to freeze within your ice.   14

Sonetto X

Le perle già di rugiadoso humore
Da l'aureo crin scotèa l'Aurora, quando
Con l'usate sue reti uscì cantando
Tirsi gentil del caro albergo fuore. 4

Tese à gli augelli, e (non sò come) Amore
Prese , che quivi alhor se n' già vagando:
Stupido, e lieto al suo prigion parlando
Disse l'accorto, e'n un saggio Pastore. 8

Amor se brami esser da me slegato
Giura di non ferirmi il cor giamai;
Ed egli, quanto vuoi prometto, e giuro. 11

Alhor Tirsi lasciollo andar securo.
Filli dolente, che più speri homai
S'hà di non saettarlo Amor giurato? 14

Sonnet 10

Already from her golden tresses Dawn
Had shaken dewy, liquid pearls when with
His usual nets, forth gentle Thyrsis came
Singing from his delightful dwelling place.[1]   4

For birds he spread his nets, but Love he caught
(I know not how), for Love lurked near at hand.
Amazed and joyful, to his prisoner
Astute words he addressed, this shepherd wise: 8

"If you desire me, Love, to set you free,
Swear to me that you'll never wound my heart."
And what he wished Love swore and promised him.   11

Thus Love let Thyrsis safely go his way.
What more, sad Phyllis, could you ever hope
Since Love had sworn he wouldn't pierce him through?   14

Madrigale V

Il mio vago homicida
Al ferir pronto, ed al sanarmi tardo
Dopo un sospirar vano,
Un desiar, un vaneggiar insano   4
Più che mai bello volge à me lo sguardo:
Poi come lampo fugge.
Così gli occhi m'abbaglia, e'l cor mi strugge.   7

All'Ill. Sig. Gabriello Chiabrera
Nessuna cosa esser più durabile della Virtù
Canzonetta Morale I

Vago di posseder l'indico argento,
O le gemme di Tiro, al falso Regno
Fida ingordo Nocchiero augel de legno
E fà, ch'ei l'ali spieghi ardito al vento.   4

Quand'ecco fremon l'onde, e Borea scorre
L'aer fosco; guerreggia ed Euro, e Noto;
Onde pieno di tema, e d'ardir voto
Egli, e sua vana speme à morte corre.   8

Fatto ricco la sete empia consola
Con l'oro quei, c'hà d'adorarlo in uso;
Ma da l'Erario in mille parti chiuso
Rapacissimo fulmine l'invola.   12

Quegli superbo tetto erger procura
Fastoso al Ciel; ma fiero il gran Tridente
Scuote Nettuno, onde veggiam repente
Tremando il suol precipitar le mura.   16

Madrigal 5

My charming murderer,
So quick to wound, but slow in healing me,
After a sighing vain,
A yearning, an insane delirium,   4
More handsome than ever turned his glance on me,
Then, like lightning, fled.
Thus my eyes he bedazzled—broke my heart.   7

To the Illustrious Mr. Gabriello Chiabrera[2]
Nothing being more lasting than Virtue
Moral Canzonetta 1

Longing to own the silver indigo
Or Tyrian gems the greedy helmsman trusts
His wooden bird upon the treacherous realm,
And boldly on the wind he spreads its wings.   4

When, lo, the waves rage and the north wind scours
The murky air; the south and southeast winds[3]
Make war, whence, filled with fear, of daring void,
He and his vain hopes both sail on to death.   8

The wicked thirst consoles those who, made rich
With gold, have grown obsessed with loving it;
But from the treasure hoard locked tight a thousand times
Most rapacious lightning snatches it.   12

Proud, ostentatious roofs Some will attempt
To raise to heaven; but Neptune fierce will shake
His trident great, whence we'll see very soon,
While the earth quakes, walls come tumbling down.[4]   16

Questi hà di Monarchia nel cor l'ambascia,
E non assonna, e toglie al corpo l'esca,
Sì di quà giù cieco desir l'invesca;
Poi l'alma spira, e i Regni ài Regni lascia.   20

Così'l Tempo distrugge, e Morte acerba
Involve nel silenzio ogni fatica
Di mortal man. la già famosa il dica
Roma, che sol di Roma il nome serba.   24

Ciò non di tè, nè di quei carmi illustri
Nobil CHIABRERA, ond'hoggi al Mondo tanto
Diletti, e giovi, il cui celeste canto
Vince d'Apollo stesso i pregi industri.   28

Ma se scherzando Clio per te rimbomba
Alto così; qual à tè gloria, e quale
A noi darà tesor ricco immortale
Di RODI, e d'AMEDEO la chiara tromba?   32

Felice quei, che l'honorato calle
Seguirà, che n'additi; e s'à le cime
Non potrà di Permesso orma sublime
Segnar; ne scorra humil la bassa Valle.   36

Di tentar fama io mai non sarò stanca
Perche'l mio nome invido oblìo non copra:
Benche m'avveggia, che sudando à l'opra
Divien pallido il volto, e'l crin s'imbianca.   40

Some have the cares of Monarchy at heart,
And do not sleep, deny the body food,
So snared (are they) by earthly blind desire;
The soul expires then; realms pass into Realms.[5]   20

So time destroys, and bitter death enshrouds
In silence every work of mortal hand;
A case in point is Rome, once so renowned,
But only the name of Rome remains in use.   24

Not, noble Chiabrera, so of you,
Nor of your glorious songs with which today
You please so, cheer the world; your heavenly song
Wins from Apollo himself the master's prize.[6]   28

But if, in jest, Clio resounds so loud[7]
Through you; what will give glory to you, what give
To us the immortal treasure rich of Rhodes
And of *Amadigi* the trumpet clear?[8]   32

Happy those who'll pursue the honored paths
You show to us, and if they can't imprint
Permessus' peak with footprints glorious,
They do not humbly creep through valleys low.[9]   36

I shall not ever tire of seeking fame,
For jealous oblivion won't obscure my name—
Although I see, while sweating at my work,
My face grow pale and my hair turning white.   40

Al medesimo
Scherzo I

Ecco l'Alba rugiadosa
Come rosa,
Sen di neve, piè d'argento,
Che la chioma inannellata
D'or fregiata
Vezzosetta sparge al vento.   6

I Ligustri, e i Gelsomini
Da' bei crini,
E dal petto alabastrino
Van cadendo; e la dolce aura
Ne ristaura
Con l'odor grato divino.   12

Febo anch'ei la chioma bionda
Fuor de l'onda
A gran passo ne discopre;
E sferzando i suoi destrieri
I pensieri
Desta in noi de l'usate opre.   18

Parte il Sonno, fugge l'ombra,
Che disgombra,
Delio già col chiaro lume
La caligine d'intorno:
Ecco il giorno,
Ond'anch'io lascio le piume.   24

E 'nfiammar mi sento il petto
Dal diletto,
Che 'n me spiran le tue Muse
Cui seguir bramo; e s'io caggio
Nel viaggio
Bel desir teco mi scuse.   30

To the same (Chiabrera)
Scherzo 1

Behold the dew-pearled dawn
So like a rose,
With snowy breast, feet silver,
Who spreads her locks of burnished gold
In ringlets curled
So charmingly on the wind.   6

The privets and the jasmine
Swirl falling
From her alabaster breast
And lovely hair; and the sweet breeze
Refreshes us
With her most welcome scent divine.   12

Phoebus also his blond hair
Reveals to us
Above the waves in one great stride.
And, when he whips his chariot's team,
In us these thoughts
Arouse our accustomed tasks.   18

Sleep takes its leave and shadows flee,
For Delius sweeps
Already with his radiant light
The mists away.[10]
The day is here,
So I too leave my feathery bed.   24

And I feel my breast inflamed
With happiness,
For in me breathe your Muses
Whom I yearn to imitate; if I
Fail on that journey,
Fine desire, with you, excuse me, please.   30

Ma s'avvien, ch'opra gentile
Dal mio stile
L'alma Clio giamai risuone:
Si dirà, sì nobil vanto
Dessi al canto
Del Ligustico Anfione.   36

Al medesimo
Che la virtù fa il vero Principe
Canzonetta Morale II

Faccia al gran Marte risonar le'ncudi
Quei, che superbo hà di regnar desìo;
Il giusto, e la ragion ponga in oblìo,
E sotto duro acciar pugnando sudi.   4

Di vincer brami, e vinca e quanto frange
Il Mar vermiglio, e'l Tigre, e'l Nilo inonda,
Patolo, Hidaspe; à cui risplende l'onda
D'oro, e di gemme, e quanto bagna il Gange.   8

Comandi à l'Indo, à l'Histro, à l'Arno, al Tago,
A la Garona, al Tebro, à l'Hermo, al Reno,
Al Danubio, à la Tana, à quanto il seno
Tocca Adige, Pò, Varo, e'l Gigeo lago.   12

Di scettro aggravi pur la destra altera,
Ciò, che brama il desir la man possegga
Chiamisi Rè, perche'l diadema regga.
Quei solo è Rè, ch'à se medesmo impera.   16

Quanti braman d'haver quà giù grandezze,
Quanti cercando van Mitre, e tesori,
Quanti di Signorie braman gli honori,
Nè san là dove sien ferme ricchezze.   20

But if a noble work results
From my technique,
Kindly Clio will rejoice always.
Then they will say: "How noble are
The things said in the song
Of this Ligurian Amphion."[11]   36

To the same (Chiabrera)
That virtue makes the true prince
Moral Canzonetta 2

With great Mars' ringing anvils let those vie
Who in their pride desire to dominate;
Justice and reason to oblivion
Let them consign and, fighting in hard steel, sweat.   4

Let him yearn to win, and let him win
Where Red Sea breaks, where Tigris, Patolus,
Nile floods—Hydaspes in whose waves gold glints
And gems; Let him win where the Ganges flows.   8

From Indus to the Istrus let him rule,
From Arno, Tagus, Tiber, Rhine, Garonne,
To Danube, Hermus, Tannus, to where the heart
Finds Adige, Po, Varus, and the Gigean Lake.[12]   12

Let even his proud right hand be burdened with
A scepter; let hand have what yearning wants.
Let him be *called* king since he wears the crown.
But only he who rules himself *is* King.   16

For grandeur in this world so many yearn,
So many vain miters seeking, treasures too,
So many the honors of a lordly rank,
Nor do they know where true wealth may be found.   20

Non argento, non or, non gemme, od ostro,
Non gli alti tetti, non le travi aurate
Fanno i Principi veri. ah più pregiate
Convengon doti in questo basso chiostro.   24

Principe è quei, che generoso affetto
Sempre hà nel cor; che sol lo sguardo porge
Là vè stuol pellegrin d'ingegni scorge,
Che sol d'alma virtù s'adorna il petto.   28

Principe è quei cui crudeltate, ò sdegno,
O vana ambizion l'alma non punge,
Che da i morsi del Volgo se n'và lunge
Non per timor, ma per sublime ingegno.   32

Tal è CINTHIO splendor del Vaticano,
Che sotto i piè l'avverso Fato hor tiene;
Onde non hà più d'oltraggiarlo spene
L'empio, di cui rende ogni studio vano.   36

E ben dimostra il tuo canoro stile
CHIABRERA illustre, che d'ogn'altro il pregio
Si lascia à dietro questo spirto egregio
Solo à se stesso di bontà simile.   40

Suo valor, e tua Musa hor tanto accenda
Ogni valor, che s'eterna al Mondo brama
Per singolar virtù candida fama
Sol da sì degno Heroe l'esempio prenda.   44

Not silver, gold, nor gems, nor purple robes,
Not lofty roofs nor rafters gilded o'er
Create real princes. Oh no, qualities
More worthy in this cloister low must meet.[13]   24

A prince is one who always in his heart
Has generous feelings, only keeps his eye
There where he spies that wise and pilgrim band
That only with generous virtue adorns its breast.   28

A prince is one whose soul is not pierced through
With vain ambition, scorn or cruelty.
Who keeps far distant from the mob's mean teeth
Not out of fear, but intellect sublime.   32

One such is Cinthio, the glory of[14]
The Vatican; he treads down adverse fate
So that the wicked one can hope to harm
No more; he foils his every vain design.   36

And brilliant Chiabrera, your tuneful style
Shows how the worth of any other's gifts is left
Behind by your distinguished soul that has
No peer in goodness but itself alone.   40

May his virtue and your muse now kindle so
Each soul that, if in the world one yearns
From a unique gift for bright, eternal fame,
Just from such heroes let him take his cue.   44

Sonetto XXIII

Del sereno mio Sol la chiara luce
(Contrario effetto) perch'io lassa viva
Quand'ella splende più, di lume priva
Fosca nel mezo dì notte m'adduce;   4

Ond'è, che versa l'una, e l'altra luce
Calde lagrime in vano, e l'Alma schiva
D'horror piena, e d'ardor di riva in riva
Mia fera stella à sospirar m'induce.   8

Sì di mia verde età misera l'hore
Traggo in pianto, e'n faville, e non comprendo
Qual sia maggior in me l'onda, ò la fiamma.   11

Tal verde legno ancor nel foco ardendo
Ne mette in dubbio, se'l cadente humore
L'incendio avanza in cui tutto s'infiamma.   14

Sonnet 23

The brilliance of my radiant sun—because
(Adverse effect) I live, ah woe, when she
Most brightly shines—cuts off my light,
And I'm transported into midnight's gloom.   4

Thus one light and the other pours hot tears
In vain; my ardent, horror-stricken soul
Recoils, and thus o'er hill and vale am I
Led sighing by my wild and savage star.   8

The wretched hours of my blooming youth I pass,
Therefore, midst tears and embers; I don't know
If water is my major trait, or flame.[15]   11

Such green, wet wood still burning in the flame
Puts that in doubt if the falling humor
Can fuel the blaze that burns up everything.   14

Sonetto XXIV

A che piango infelice? à che sospiro?
Ah questi indizi son d'usata doglia.
Al pianto, ed à i sospiri il fren discioglia
Quei, ch'amando sostien lieve martiro.   4

Troppo del sen, troppo de gli occhi usciro
Sospiri, e pianti. hor che più fier m'addoglia
Il mio tormento di morir m'invoglia
Disperato, e giustissimo desiro.   8

Se non m'ancide il duol, se'nvan m'attempo
Per impetrar mercè del lungo affanno
Deh qual salute homai sperar mi lice?   11

Sciogli tu Morte pia que' nodi, c'hanno
Quest'Alma avvinta; che'l morir à tempo
È don dato dal Cielo, e don felice.   14

Sonnet 24

Why do I weep unhappy? Sigh for what?
Ah, these are symptoms of accustomed woe.
Let one who, loving, lightly bears the pain
Yield up the reins to weeping and to sighs.   4

Sighs issued from my breast too often, tears
Too many from my eyes flowed forth since now
With death I, desperate, have fallen in love,
And very justly I desire to die.   8

If sorrow doesn't kill me, if in vain
I age through begging mercy for long woe,
Ah, for what health ever may I rightly hope?   11

O kindly Death, untie those knots that have
Enmeshed this soul; for it is Heaven's gift
To die when time is right—a happy gift.   14

Sonetto XXV

Già vidi occhi leggiadri, occhi, ond'Amore
M'incende, in voi bella pietà scolpita
Che dolce lusingando al mio dolore,
Al mio fido servir promise aita.   4

Hor veggio (lassa) il troppo folle errore
D'ingannato pensier, d'alma tradita;
Veggio, che discacciata (ohime) dal core
La pietade ne gli occhi era fuggita.   8

O sospirati in van dolci riposi
Quali havranno i miei giorni hore tranquille?
Qual guiderdone i miei martiri ascosi?   11

Deh potessero almeno in voi le stille
De l'amaro mio pianto occhi amorosi
Quel, che possono in me vostre faville.   14

Sonnet 25

I once saw charming eyes, saw eyes whence Love
Enkindled me, saw lovely pity carved
In you. That sweet illusion, to my grief,
For my devoted service promised aid.   4

Now, woe, I see the foolish error of
A thought deluded, of a soul betrayed;
I see that pity, exiled from the heart,
Had fled away, alas, into the eyes.   8

O you vainly longed-for respites sweet,
Which of my days will have a tranquil hour?
And what will recompense my hidden pangs?   11

Ah, if only the drops of my embittered tears,
Of my enamored eyes, could cause in you
That which your sparkling embers caused in me.   14

Sonetto XXVI

Quando Sdegno gli sproni aspri, e pungenti
Mi pone al fianco il cor di te si duole;
Ond'io formo i concetti, e le parole
Da sfogar teco i duri miei lamenti;   4

Ma come al gran soffiar de' maggior venti
Caliginosa Nube fuggir suole:
Così nel tuo apparir vago mio Sole
Parte lo sdegno, e fuggono i tormenti.   8

Se di lagnarmi poi prendo consiglio
Finisco al cominciar le gravi offese,
E ride il cor quand'è severo il ciglio.   11

Madre così qualhor tremante rese
Con le minaccie il pargoletto figlio
Tanto l'accarezzò, quanto l'offese.   14

Madrigale IX

Per lo soverchio affanno
Gli miei spirti dolenti
Abbandonato m'hanno;
E i sensi, che già fur di fiamma ardenti.   4
Freddo ghiaccio si fanno;
Ond'io chiudo le luci, e mi scoloro,
E crede Amor, ch'io dorma, & io pur moro.   7

Sonnet 26

When with its sharp and cruel spurs Disdain
Rakes hard my flank, my heart complains of you;
On this account I shape conceits and words
For venting with you my embittered tears.   4

But just as misty clouds are wont to flee
Before the bluster of great winds—just so
At your appearance, O my lovely Sun,
Disdain departs, and all my torments flee.   8

If I should then decide to vent my grief
I end at their beginning these grave harms,
And, though the brow's severe, the heart still smiles—   11

As when a mother who with threats has set
Her tiny son atremble, just as much
As she had done him harm, caressed him then.   14

Madrigal 9

For overwhelming woe
These sorrowful spirits of mine
Have quite abandoned me;
My senses too, already burnt with flame   4
Have frozen into ice;
On this account my lights I close, grow pale;
Love thinks I'm sleeping, but in fact I die.   7

Sonetto XXXVII

O De l'Anima mia nobil tesoro
Tu pur risplendi à i boschi, à i monti, à i rivi,
Che pregiar non ti pon di ragion privi
Mentr'io quì sola e mi querelo, e ploro.   4

Deh torna à me, che'l tuo bel viso adoro
E lunge scaccia i pensier gravi, e schivi;
Fuggi gli horrori, ov'à mio danno hor vivi,
E me consola, che languendo moro.   8

Rasciuga gli occhi homai dal pianger lassi.
Ahi che le Fere ti faran più fiero
S'ivi più tardi, e viè più freddo l'onde.   11

Più selvaggio le selve e'l cor' altero
In cui durezza natural s'asconde
In sasso al fin si cangierà tra' sassi.   14

Sonnet 37

O noble treasure of my soul, on woods you shine
Still, on the mountains, on the streams; they can't
Praise you as they lack reason. Meanwhile I,
Alone, am weeping and lamenting here.   4

Return to me, for I adore your face
So lovely; drive my dull, grave thoughts away;
Flee horrors where, to my harm, now, you dwell;
Console me, because languishing I die.   8

The tears you left, from my eyes wipe at last.
Woe lest the wild beasts make you fiercer still
If you delay, if waves are colder there.   11

More savage than the woods, that haughty heart
Where hardness natural conceals itself
In stone until, at last, heart turns to stones.   14

Sonetto XXXVIII

Mentre quasi liquor tutto bollente
Il liquefatto vetro à la man cede,
Qual più brama l'Artefice prudente
Forma vaga, e gentil prender si vede.   4

Così mentre vivesti entro l'ardente
Fiamma, ch'io già destai, forma ti diede
Amor più, ch'altro mai Fabro possente
De la tanto appo lui gradita fede.   8

Ma come perde ogni calor in breue
Il fragil vetro, e di leggier si spezza
Spargendo al fin l'altrui fatiche à terra,   11

Così de la tua fè l'ardor fù lieve,
Debil percossa poi d'altra bellezza
Spezzolla e'l mio sperar chiuse sotterra.   14

Sonnet 38

While almost liquid, all aboil, then glass
That's liquefied is molded in one's hand
Just as the careful craftsman most desires
And one sees lovely, noble form take shape. 4

Thus while you lived amidst the burning flame
That I once set ablaze, Love gave you form
More pleasing than could ever be, compared
With his, another able craftsman's work. 8

But just as fragile glass soon loses all
Its heat, and shatters easily at last,
Scattering its maker's labors on the ground, 11

So was the ardor of your faith but slight;
Another beauty's weak blow shattered it
And then entombed my hope beneath the earth. 14

Sonetto XXXIX

Morfeo gentil se nel mostrarmi solo
Benigno il bel sembiante, ond'io tant'anni
Hò pianto, han pace i miei sì lunghi affanni,
Perche si tosto (ohime) te n' fuggi à volo?   4

Deh per pietà del mi' angoscioso duolo
Spiega di novo à mio soccorso i vanni;
Ch'à l'apparir de' tuoi graditi inganni
Sgombra de' miei martir l'antico stuolo;   8

E se pur di lasciarmi al fin agogni,
E'nsieme ancor se' di gradirmi vago,
Non far ritorno à la cimeria sede;   11

Ma scuopri questa mia pallida Imago
Al mio Signor ne' suoi notturni sogni;
Ch'à te creder potria s'à me non crede.   14

Madrigale XIII

Quest'empia Donna altera,
Che m'hà dal petto il tristo cor disciolto
Perpetua Primavera   3
Hà nel leggiadro voltô:
Ma perch'io viva in un tormento eterno
Nel sen poi chiude tempestoso Verno.   6

Sonnet 39

Sweet Morpheus, if you are only kind
In showing me that lovely face—for which long years
I've wept—so my long woes find peace, why do
You rather flee (alas!) in flight from me?　　　　4

Ah, for pity of my agonizing woe,
Again spread wide, for my relief, your wings;
For at the coming of your welcome frauds,
My ancient troop of sufferings clears off;　　　　8

And though you yearn to leave me in the end
Yet, at the same time, still would grant a boon,
Do not return to your high-towered seat;　　　　11

Reveal, instead, my pallid image in
His nightly dreaming to my Lord; for he
Can believe you though he won't believe me.　　　　14

Madrigal 13

This wicked lady proud
Who has unchained my sad heart from my breast
Has spring perpetual　　　　3
In her delightful face:
But so I'll live in never-ending pain,
She then keeps stormy winter in her breast.　　　　6

Madrigale XV

A l'apparir del Sole
La neve in liquid'onde
Per sua natura distillar si suole.   3
Io (lassa) quando il mio bel Sol s'asconde
Verso da gli occhi tanto
Humor, che tutta mi distillo in pianto.   6

Sestina I

Misera pria sarà calda la neve,
E sorgerà dal Mar Febo la sera,
E fiori produrran le secche piante,
Ed Echo sarà muta à gli altrui versi,
Che la nemica mia contraria sorte
Resti un dì sol di tormentarmi il core.   6

Nè sia mai, che la fiammma del mio core
Tempri di quell'altier la fredda neve.
Piangerò dunque (ahi dispietata sorte)
Da un'alba à l'altra, e d'una à l'altra sera;
E con gli afflitti miei ruvidi versi
Andrò noiando e Fere, e Sassi, e Piante.   12

Tante frondi non son per queste piante
Quant'io porto saette affisse al core;
Nè fede può, nè servitù, nè versi,
Nè l'arder (lassa) à la più algente neve,
Nè'l vedermi languir mattino, e sera
Far, che'ei muti pensiero, io cangi sorte.   18

Madrigal 15

At the Sun's appearance,
Snow by its nature is
Disposed to be distilled to liquid waves.   3
But I, alas, when my fair sun's concealed,
Shed so much liquid from
My eyes that I'm entirely turned to tears.   6

Sestina 1

Ah wretched one, all blistering will snow
Become, and Phoebus from the sea will rise at eve,
And flowers be produced from dried-out plants,
And Echo will keep still at others' verse
Before my enemy, my adverse fate,
Will cease tormenting, just one day, my heart.   6

Nor ever will the flame that's in my heart
Be lessened by that lofty, cooling snow;
Thus I shall weep (Alas, unpitying fate)
From one dawn to another, from one eve
Until the next, and in my rugged verse
Vex with my heartaches beasts and stones and plants.   12

There aren't as many leaves upon these plants[16]
As I bear arrows fixed within my heart;
And neither faith, nor servitude, nor verse,
Nor burning love (woe!) on that frigid snow,
Nor seeing me in anguish morn and eve,
Can change his mind or let me change my fate.   18

Perch'altri intenda la mia fiera sorte
Scriverò per li sassi, e per le piante,
Che'al nascer del mio dì giunse la sera
Colpa di lui, ch'eternamente il core
Portò coperto d'indurata neve
Non curando'l mio duol, l'amore, o i versi.   24

Traggon dal Ciel la fredda Luna i versi,
Rendon benigna altrui l'iniqua sorte,
Fanno da calde fiamme uscir la neve,
Fermar l'onde fugaci, andar le piante,
Cangiar il chiaro giorno in fosca sera
Per me render non puon men' aspro un core.   30

Morendo vive per mia doglia il core,
Parlando perdo le parole, e i versi,
Rido piangendo, e'l dì vado, e la sera
Pascendo l'alma in così dura sorte;
E voi sapete la mia fede ò piante
Superar di candor la pura neve.   36

Ma se di neve un'agghiacciato core
Scaldar non puon per queste piante i versi
Giunga ò mia sorte homai l'ultima sera.   39

Madrigale XVII

Amor d'amor ardea
De la vezzosa, e bella
Amorosa Nigella;
Ed à lei come à riverita Dea   4
(Lasso) fè sacrifizio del mio core.
Ahi sorte iniqua, e rea.
Di Nigella è l'honore.
Di Cupido la gloria, e mio'l dolore.   8

So others may comprehend my savage fate,
On stones I shall compose, write on the plants,
For at the birth of my day came its eve;
The fault is his who always bears his heart
Encased forever in unmelting snow;
He cares not for my sorrow, love, or verse.   24

The cold moon from the sky is drawn by verse;
Verse makes grow kindly someone's wicked fate,
And from the searing flames verse causes snow
To fall, stops fleeing waves, (and) makes plants walk,
Makes shining day transform to dusky eve;
Less hard toward me it cannot make his heart.   30

Alive while dying for sorrow is my heart;
Though speaking I lose the words as well as verse;
I, weeping, laugh; I pace both day and eve
While nourishing my soul with this hard fate;
And you know that my constancy, O plants,
In purity surpasses driven snow.   36

But if, because of snow, an icy heart
Cannot be warmed by these plants or this verse,
O never, my fate, let come the final eve.   39

Madrigal 17

Love was aflame with love
For lovely, amorous,
And sweet Nigella;
To her (alas) he sacrificed my heart   4
As to a goddess whom one holds in awe.
Oh wicked, evil fate!
The honor is Nigella's
Cupid's the glory, mine the woe.   8

Sonetto XLVI

Qual travagliata Nave io mi raggìro
Senza governo in tempestoso Mare:
Nè veggio chi le tenebre rischiare
Del mio dolor, nè alcun soccorso miro;   4

E'ncontr'al Cielo à gran ragion m'adìro,
Poi ch'Orion sol per me (lassa) appare;
E mi s'ascondon le bramate, e chiare
Luci de i figli, che di Leda uscìro.   8

Crescono ogn'hor le horribili procelle,
L'aer tutte le'ngiurie, e i furor suoi
Mostra contra'l mio stanco afflitto legno.   11

Aura'l tuo fiato sia, sien gli occhi stelle
Sia porto il seno, ch'io non curo poi
Di Nettuno, e del Ciel tempesta, ò sdegno.   14

Capitolo I. Con ogni terzo verso del Petrarca

Lunge da le tue luci alme, e divine
Impossibil sarà, ch'io fuggir possa
L'hore del pianto, che son già vicine.   3

D'ogni letizia la mia fronte è scossa.
Ahi destin crudo, ahi mia nemica sorte
Hor hai fatto l'estremo di tua possa.   6

Deh chi m'insegna le mie fide scorte,
Deh chi m'insegna (ohime) dove dimora
Mio ben, mio male, mia vita, e mia morte?   9

Mi sento venir men più d'hora in hora,
Anzi giunger al fin de la mia vita,
Tanto cresce'l desio, che m'innamora.   12

Sonnet 46

Just like a storm-tossed ship I'm whirled about,
Without a rudder in a turbulent sea;
I see none who the darkness of my woe
Can brighten, and no rescue I expect.   4

Against heaven with good reason I'm enraged,
Since for me Orion only (woe!) appears;
From me are hid the yearned-for, shining lights
Of those twin children born from Leda's womb.[17]   8

These awful tempests grow with every hour;
The winds are buffeting everything; they vent
Their fury on my weary, battered barque.   11

Let your breath be the breeze, your eyes the stars,
And your breast be the port, then I won't care
For Neptune, and Heaven's tempest I'll disdain.   14

Capital 1. With every third line by Petrarch

Far distant from your kindly, heavenly eyes
It won't be possible for me to flee
The hours for tears, already near at hand.[18]   3

From every delight my face is turned away.
Alas, cruel destiny; Oh fate, my foe,
Now you have done the worst within your power.[19]   6

What trusty escorts, ah, will show my way?
Ah who will teach me (woe) where these may dwell:
My weal, my harm, my life, my death as well?[20]   9

I feel myself grow fainter hour by hour—
Feel rather the approach of my life's end,
So great grows the passion that makes me fall in love.[21]   12

Chi sia che possa darmi breve aita,
Se nel partir del mio vivace Sole
È l'aura mia vital da me partita?   15

Mi stanno al cor l'angeliche parole,
E l'accorte maniere, e'l dolce riso,
Tal che di rimembrar mi giova, e duole.   18

Ahi mentre penso, che da me diviso
T'hà l'empio Amor, perch'io morendo viva
Piovommi amare lagrime dal viso.   21

Io vò cercando ogn'hor di riva in riva,
Nè trovar posso l'amoroso obbietto,
Di cui convien, che'n tante carte scriva.   24

Movono fieri assalti à questo petto
Noiose cure, e sol me resta (ahi Fato)
Lagrimar sempre il mio sommo diletto.   27

S'io temo, che'l mio ben mi sia'nvolato,
S'io temo, ch'egli altrove pieghi'l core
Questo temer d'antiche prove è nato.   30

Spero s'havrà pietà del mio dolore,
Ch'è fuor'ogn'altro dispietato, e fiero
Ove sia chi per prova intenda amore.   33

Ben veggio (lassa) e non m'inganna il vero,
Che già gran tempo io posi per costui
Egualmente in non cale ogni pensiero.   36

Mentre vivendo in potestate altrui
Potei godere il desiato volto
Tremando, ardendo assai felice fui.   39

Ma poi, ch'à gli occhi il grato cibo è tolto,
Nè senton quest'orecchie i cari accenti
Quant'io veggio m'è noia, e quant'io ascolto.   42

Who is there that could bring me hasty aid
If, when I part from my life-giving sun,
The breeze that brings me life were gone from me?[22]   15

Those words angelic rest within my heart,
And that good-natured manner, that sweet smile,
So that recalling brings me joy, and woe.[23]   18

Ah when, I think how wicked Love, has torn
You from me, so that, dying, I'm alive,
What bitter tears fall raining from my face.[24]   21

Each hour I wander searching from shore to shore,
But that beloved object I can't find
Of whom, on many pages, I must write.[25]   24

Vexatious cares mount fierce assaults upon
This breast, and all that's left for me (ah, Fate)
Is weeping forever, my supreme delight.[26]   27

If I fear my good from me will be purloined,
If I fear he'll elsewhere bend his heart,
This terror has been born from ancient trial.[27]   30

I hope I shall be pitied for my woe,
Which past all else is merciless and fierce,
By someone seasoned in the ways of love.[28]   33

I see well, and (alas) I'm not deceived
By truth, that for a long time—for this man—
Each care I have neglected equally.[29]   36

While I was living in that other's power,
I could enjoy that longed-for countenance;
Aflame, atremble, I was most content.[30]   39

But then, when from my eyes the yearned-for food
Was snatched, and my ears heard not those accents dear,
Whatever I saw or heard exhausted me.[31]   42

Forman le voci mie gravi lamenti,
E'ntanto questi abbandonati lidi
Vò misurando à passi tardi, e lenti.   45

Quest'aria'ngombro di noiosi stridi,
E gli occhi volgo per mirar s'io veggio
Luoghi da sospirar riposti, e fidi.   48

Se vinta dal dolor piango, e vaneggio,
S'io vivo sempre in amorosi guai
La mia Fortuna che mi può far peggio?   51

Deh cessa Amor di travagliarmi homai,
Rivolgi altrove il tuo dorato strale,
Ch'io mi pasco di lagrime, e tu'l sai.   54

Il tanto seguitarmi al fin che vale?
Deh lascia il tormentarmi à que' begli occhi,
Che'l foco del mio cor fanno immortale.   57

Par ben, ch'ogni sventura à me sol tocchi,
Ond'à ragion quest'Anima dolente
Avvien, che'n pianto, ò'n lamentar trabocchi.   60

Quando respirerà mia stanca mente?
Quando sia mai, che riveder io speri
Gli occhi, di ch'io parlai sì caldamente?   63

Occhi del mio morir ministri fieri
Non vi celate, ò'n tanta guerra almeno
Datemi pace ò duri miei pensieri.   66

O quanta invidia porto à quel terreno
Dove resplendon quei vivaci lumi,
Che fanno intorno à se l'aer sereno.   69

Bench'amando, e servendo io mi consumi,
Amerò, servito lunge, e dappresso
Mentre, che al Mar discenderanno i fiumi.   72

My words are fashioning my grave laments,
And meanwhile I wander these forsaken shores,
Measuring them with lagging paces slow.[32]   45

This air I burden with my dreary cries,
And turn my eyes to gaze if I espy
Places secluded and safe for breathing sighs.[33]   48

If overcome by grief I weep and rave,
If I forever live in amorous woe,
How can my fortune treat me any worse?[34]   51

Ah, Love, desist henceforth from troubling me;
Your gilded arrows aim some other way;
I feed myself on tears as you well know.[35]   54

From so pursuing me, what gain at last?
Ah, leave off torturing me with those fine eyes
That make the fire immortal in my heart.[36]   57

Every misfortune seems to touch just me,
And so in reason this dejected soul
Should overflow with weeping or lament.[37]   60

When will my weary mind find space to breathe?
When may I ever hope to see again
Those eyes I spoke so passionately of?[38]   63

O eyes, you savage heralds of my death,
Don't hide yourselves; in such great war at least,
My unrelenting cares, O grant me peace.[39]   66

Oh what great envy for that land I feel,
There where those lively lights so brightly glow
They make the air around them shine serene.[40]   69

Though in loving and in serving I'm consumed,
I'll love and serve both near-by and afar
As long as to the sea the streams flow down.[41]   72

Che viva il cor da tante pene oppresso,
Ch'io viva, e spiri in così gravi affanni
Meco di me mi meraviglio spesso.   75

Ohime, che l'hore, i giorni, i mesi, e gli anni
Consumo invan quest'Anima mi dice
Trista, e certa indovina de' miei danni.   78

Ben son io ne' martir sola Fenice,
E tù lo vedi, e ne gioisci, e godi
O del dolce mio mal prima radice.   81

Sì stretti sono gli amorosi nodi
Co' quali Amore il cor mi stringe intorno,
Che Morte sola fia, ch'indi lo snodi.   84

Deh verrà mai quel desiato giorno,
In cui possa fruir quant'io vorrei
La dolce vista del bel viso adorno?   87

Crudel à che non torni? à che non bei
Me di quel bel, per cui tutt'altro oblio?
Ma tù prendi à diletto i dolor miei   90

E i sospiri, e le lagrime, e'l desio.

That my heart lives oppressed by such great pains,
That I live in such grave distress and breathe,
Within, I marvel often at myself.[42]   75

Oh me, that hours, days, and months, and years
I waste in vain—this says my soul to me—
Unerring, sad diviner of my loss.[43]   78

Yes, I'm a lonely Phoenix in my pangs;
You see it, revel in it, relish it,
O root of my first sweet iniquity.[44]   81

The amorous knots with which Love has enmeshed
My heart completely are so tightly pulled
That only Death can loose me from its toils.[45]   84

Ah when will ever come that longed-for day
On which I can enjoy as I would wish
The sweet sight of that handsome, comely face.[46]   87

Why, cruel one, don't you return, why not
Bless me with those good looks for which I shun
All others? But my sorrows you enjoy,[47]   90

My sighs, my tears, and my desire as well.[48]

Sonetto XLVII

Tirsi dolce mio ben se dal valore,
Onde sì illustre, e glorioso vai
Nasce quest'amor mio, nascono i guai,
M'è soàve'l languir, dolce l'ardore.   4

Se da l'amato angelico splendore
Di quei duo soli amorosetti, e gài
Movon gli strali, onde ferita m'hai,
E de le piaghe mie dolce il dolore.   8

Se da la bocca, e dal soàve riso
Le mie lagrime nascono, e i sospiri,
M'è'l pianger dolce, e'l sospirar m'è grato.   11

Dunque vivrò ne' dolci miei martiri,
E'l cor, che dolcemente fù piagato
Per morte ancor non sia da te diviso.   14

Madrigale XVIII

O Lagrime, ch'ad arte
Hò tante volte sparte in questo Rìo,
Lagrime in cui s'asconde il foco, ond'io
Mi struggo à parte, à parte
Quando talhor bagnate   5
Le delicate membra
Di colei, che del Ciel Diva rassembra
Dite lagrime ingrate
Perche de l'amor mio non l'infiammate?   9

Sonnet 47

My Thyrses sweet, though it is from that worth
Whence so illustrious and glorious you come,
This love of mine is born, my woes are born;
The languor is ease to me, the ardor sweet.   4

If from the belovèd radiance, angel-like,
Of those two bright, flirtatious suns there fly
The arrows with which I've been wounded so,
The sorrow of my injuries is sweet.   8

If from the mouth and from the gentle smile
My tears are born, my sighs as well,
The sighs delight me, the sweet weeping's mine.   11

Then I shall live in my sweet suffering,
My heart, too, that was sweetly wounded will
Not even by death be torn away from you.   14

Madrigal 18

O tears that artfully
I many times have scattered in this stream,
You tears in whom that fire is hid with which
I am consumed by inches,
When you sometimes bathe   5
Her limbs so delicate—
Hers who is like a goddess come from Heaven—
Say, you ungrateful tears,
Why do you not inflame her with my love?   9

Madrigale XIX

Dopo la pioggia del mio pianto amaro
Come sovente ei suole
M'apparve il mio bel Sole
Più de l'usato chiaro: 4
Al cui raggio improviso
Di più colori mi si tinse il viso;
Ond'Iride novella io son'intanto
In virtù del suo lume, e del mio pianto.   8

Sonetto XLIX

Quando alluma nascendo il Sol la terra,
E l'horror de le tenebre sparisce,
S'allegra il bosco, e'l prato rifiorisce,
Ride la rosa, e l'ostro suo disserra;   4

Ma s'ei s'avanza, e quasi armato in guerra
Vibra'l raggio possente, e'l suol ferisce
Ella, che già ridèa mesta languisce,
E l'ostro cade impallidito à terra.   8

Così chi diede pur vita, e vaghezza
Dianzi al purpureo fior cangiando tempre
D'honor lo spoglia, anzi fà sì, ch'ei muore.   11

Tal pria nascendo entro'l mio seno Amore
Sparse l'anima, e i sensi di dolcezza
Cresciuto hor fà, che'n troppo ardor mi stempre.   14

Madrigal 19

After the rainfall of my bitter tears,
As he so often does
My lovely sun appeared to me
Brighter than usual;   4
At his unexpected ray
My face grew flushed with many colored hues;
And so, since then, new Iris I've become
By virtue of his light, and of my tears.[49]   8

Sonnet 49

When the rising sun lights up the earth
And the horrors of the darkness disappear,
The woods rejoice and meadows bloom again,
The rose laughs, and her petals open wide;   4

If the sun, though, grows oppressive, almost armed
For war, and brandishes his mighty rays[50]
And wounds the earth, she who once laughed will wilt,
And, ashen, her petals fall upon the earth.   8

Thus, he who once before gave life and joy
To a purple flower, by changing moods strips it
Of honor, in fact behaves so that it dies.   11

So formerly Love rising in my breast
Set free my soul—the sense of sweetness too—
Now Love grown great melts me with too much heat.   14

Scherzo II

Io credeà, che trà gli amanti
Solo i pianti,
Sol l'angosce, sol le pene
Senza spene fosser quelle
Rie procelle
Turbatrici d'ogni bene.   6

Io credèa, che'nfausta sorte
Doglia, e morte
Sostenesse un cor lontano
Da la mano, che'l saetta,
Che l'aletta,
Per cui piange, e stride in vano.   12

Io credeà, quando sdegnose
Le amorose
Luci il vago afflitto mira,
E sospira, fosse questa
Pena infesta
Sol cagion di sdegno, e d'ira.   18

Io credeà, che'n fier tormento
Il contento
Si cangiasse d'un'amante,
Che'l sembiante amato perde,
Onde'l verde
Fugge al fin di speme errante.   24

E stimai, che senza essempio
Fosse l'empio
Fato (ohime) di quel dolente,
Che languente non hà pace,
E si sface
Ne l'incendio vanamente.   30

Scherzo 2

I used to think, among these lovers, that
There could be naught
But weeping only, anguish,
Only hopeless pain amidst
Vile hurricanes,
Disrupters of every good.   6

I used to think ill-omened fate,
Sorrow, and death
A heart would undergo
Far distant from the hand
That with an arrow pierces it,
That charms it so,
For which it weeps and cries out all in vain.   12

I thought that when the lovely, smitten one
Looks on those lights,
Scornful and amorous,
And sighs, this grievous pain
Alone would be
The only cause of wrath and of disdain.   18

I thought that into torment fierce
The happiness
Would change of one who loves,
But loses the beloved face,
Whence in the end
The springtime's errant hope will flee.   24

I judged too that unparalleled
The wicked fate
Would be (Oh!) of that woeful one
Who, grieving, finds no peace
And is undone
With burning pointlessly.   30

Ma godendo non pensai,
Che trar guai
Da sue gioie un cor devesse,   '
O potesse nel gioire
Sì languire,
Ch'a doler d'Amor s'havesse.   36

Nè credeà, ch'amante amato
Del suo stato
Sospirasse: hor da l'effetto
Da l'affetto provo, Amore,
Che'l dolore
Segue sempre il tuo diletto.   42

Stringa pur l'amato collo,
Che satollo
Mai non sia quei, che ben ama;
Perche brama il bel celeste
Chiuso in queste
Membra, e'nvan lo cerca, e brama.   48

O d'amor sorte infelice
Se non lice
Mai gioir. tue cure ponno
(Fero donno) scure, e chiare,
Dolci, amare
Torne dunque il cibo, e'l sonno?   54

But, rejoicing, I'd not thought
That from its joys
A heart would have to draw its woes,
Or could, in finding joy,
So languish that
It would have to complain of love.   36

Nor did I think a lover who was loved
Would sigh about
His state: now by the consequence,
By the desire, O Love, I prove
That sad remorse
Forever follows your delight.   42

Hug tight, then, the beloved neck,
For never will
Those have their fill who truly love;
For one who yearns for loveliness
Celestial, in earthly limbs
Seeks it out and yearns for it in vain.   48

O wicked fate, if never one
Can righteously
Rejoice for love—since light and dark
your cares (a savage lord) impose,
Both sweet and bitter too—
When, then, will sleep and appetite return?   54

Madrigale XX

O Bellissimo petto
Dolce petto amoroso
De l'avido mio sguardo altero oggetto
Per questo caldo humore,   4
Ond'hor se' rugiadoso
Poiche partir convien rendimi il core.
Nò nò. sia meglio, ch'io nel duol mi stempre
Pur che'n si degno albergo ei viva sempre.   8

Alla Sereniss. Sig. D. Virginia Medici D'Este
Duchessa di Modena, etc.
Sonetto LVII

Se da le Sfere, onde'l valor prendeste
Donna, e'l bel guardo alteramente humile
Tolt'eguale havess'io canoro stile
Vostra lode per me forse udireste.   4

Ma l'alte doti, e le bellezze honeste
Gradito ardor d'ogni anima gentile
Potrieno haver terreno carme à vile,
Che sol degno è di lor canto celeste.   8

Dunque bella d'Heroe figlia, e consorte
Quel, ch'io non posso, e che pur dir vorrei
Risuonino per me l'eterne Rote.   11

Chi vi diè la virtù spiegar la puote.
Hor dica'l Cielo in chiare voci, e scorte
Non luce in me quel, che non splende in lei.   14

Madrigal 20

O you most lovely breast,
O sweet breast amorous,
You lofty object of my avid gaze,
By these scalding tears   4
With which you're now bedewed,
Since you must part, restore my heart to me.
No, no. Better I dissolve in woe so that
In such a lodging fine he'll ever dwell.   8

To the most serene lady Duchess Virginia Medici D'Este
Duchess of Modena, etc.
Sonnet 57

If from the spheres whence you took valor, Lady,
And took that fair and proudly humble glance,
I equally had taken lyric style,
From me your praises you'd perhaps have heard.   4

But your high qualities and beauty chaste,
The ardor pleasing to every noble soul
Can have just earthly and low melodies
Though only celestial song is fit for them.   8

Therefore, O Hero's consort and fair child,
That which I'd like to say, though I cannot,
Let the eternal wheels sing out for me.   11

Your virtue they who gave it can explain.
Oh, now let Heaven say in clear, plain words:
"No light's in me that doesn't shine in her."   14

Madrigale XXIV

Vide Lesbin Nisida sua fugace
Armar di strali un die
La delicata mano;
E disse alhor, perche non trovin pace   4
Amor le angosce mie
Fiero porgi quell'armi e non in vano
A quella man, perch'emula de gli occhi
Dentro à l'anima mia saette scocchi.   8

Scherzo V

Care gioie,
Che le noie
De' sospir mandate in bando.
Quel diletto,
C'hò nel petto
Scopran gli occhi sfavillando.   6

Hor non finge,
Hor non pinge
Con sua squadra falsa, e vaga
Sogno Vano
Quella mano,
Che si dolce il sen m'impiaga.   12

Bell'avorio
Pur mi glorio',
Che per mille dardi, e faci,
Che m'aventi
Hor consenti,
Ch'io ti porga mille baci.   18

Madrigal 24

Lesbin saw his Nisida flee away[51]
Saw her delicate hand
Armed with darts one day;
And he said then: "Why don't my pangs, O Love,   4
Find any peace at all?
Fierce one, you put those weapons in that hand—
Not vainly—since it rivals arrows that
From those eyes you let fly into my soul."   8

Scherzo 5

Precious pleasures,
Into exile
All of sighing's cares you banish.
This delight
That's in my breast
Those sparkling eyes are making clear.   6

Now Sleep tricks not
Now depicts not
With his false and charming troop,
In idle dream
The winsome hand
That so sweetly wounds my breast.   12

O fair ivory,
My sure glory,
Just for the thousand fiery darts
That I've suffered,
Now consent that
I kiss you a thousand times.   18

Fresche rose
Ove pose
D'Ibla il mel cortese Amore
Pur delibo
Grato cibo
Premio altier del mio dolore.   24

Parolette
Vezzosette
Per cui già beàr mi sento
Pur v'ascolto,
Nè m'è tolto
Da l'Aurora il mio contento.   30

Frena, frena
Lingua piena
Di piacer la tua dolcezza:
Sai l'Aurora
S'innamora,
Ed è scaltra à furti avezza.   36

Ma Vaneggio
Me n'aveggio
Belle Ninfe ella non toglie.
Ah pur Giove
Non ritrove
Forma nova, e me ne spoglie.   42

O rosebuds fresh
Where kindly Love
Fair Hybla's honey sweet has set,[52]
At last I taste
That welcome food,
My woe's lofty recompense. 24

Witty sayings,
Sweet endearments
By which I feel blessed, indeed,
Yes, I hear you,
And Aurora[53]
Will not steal my happiness. 30

Curb, O curb you,
Tongue so brimming
With your pleasures sweet; you know
Aurora might
Enamored grow,
And one had better watch her thieving ways. 36

But I'm raving,
I feel certain
Pretty nymphs she will not steal.
Ah, but might Jove
Not discover
Some new form—snatch her from me? 42

Madrigale XXIX

Và pur lasso mio core
Và pur core à colei,
C'hor avviva, hor ancide i pensier miei,
E dille quanto sopportiam' dolore
Per la sua feritate;   5
E s'ella nega al tuo languir pietate
A me ritorna; e se ritrovi, ch'io
Sia giunto al fin del mesto viver mio,
Piangi l'aspra mia sorte,
E dì, che troppo amando io giunsi à morte.   10

Madrigale XXXIII

Amor se con leggiadro, e novo inganno
Hai per tuo segno eletto
Questo misero petto,   3
Almen, perche'l mio danno
Non veggia quando in me gli strali scocchi,
Velami per pietà, velami gli occhi.   6

Scherzo VI

A Che sguardi amorosetti
Tanti petti
Saettar? deh per pietate
Più non siate altrui cortesi
De gli accesi
Raggi ardenti, onde beàte.   6

Madrigal 29

Go hence my heart, alas,
My heart, go hence to her
Who quickens now my thoughts now deadens them;
And tell her how much sorrow we endure
Because she's so untamed;   5
And if she won't take pity on your woe,
Come back to me; and if you find that I
Have come to the end of my unhappy life
Weep for my cruel fate,
And say I died because I loved too much.   10

Madrigal 33

O Love, if with some charming, new deceit
You've picked this wretched breast
To be your target, O   3
At least don't let me see
My harm when you are shooting darts in me;
For pity's sake, blindfold me; veil my eyes!   6

Scherzo 6

Why, O you flirtatious glances,
Do you pierce
So many breasts? For pity's sake, ah,
No more let others share the favors
Of the ardent,
Burning rays with which you bless.   6

Pupillete nel cui lampo
Sempre avampo
Se mia gioia è'n voi raccolta
Deh sia volta à me la face,
Che mi sface,
C'hà da me l'alma disciolta.   12

Se bramate le facelle
Chiare Stelle
Per men mal temprar ne i pianti
De gli amanti: gli ampi fiumi
De' miei lumi
Godan sol sì alteri vanti.   18

Se volete luci vaghe
Mille piaghe
Rimirar: deh sia l'honore
Del mio core: in cui vedrete
Luci liete
Quante havèa saette Amore.   24

Mostr'io pur quanto pungenti,
Quanto ardenti
L'auree fiamme, gli aurei dardi
Cari sguardi sono. hor basti.
Non più fasti
Lampi in un vaghi, e bugiardi.   30

Voi giurate scintillando,
Fiammeggiando,
Che del pianto, e del mio male
Pur vi cale. indi le palme
Di mill'alme
Brama il foco, ama lo strale.   36

Charming pupils in whose flashing
I blaze ever,
If my joy is gathered in you,
Ah, upon me turn your torch;
It undoes me,
For it's stripped my soul from me.   12

If, bright stars, you yearn for sparks
For tempering
Lover's tears to ease their ills,
Such haughty boasts alone rejoice
At rivers
Overflowing from my lights.   18

If, lovely lights, it's your desire
To look upon
A thousand wounds, ah, let it be
The honor of my heart, wherein
You'll see, blithe lights,
How many arrows Love can own.   24

I'll show you just how many are
My wounds, how flames
Of gold and golden darts can sear,
O precious glances; now enough—
No longer vex
Sweet lamps and liars all in one.   30

All asparkle you are vowing,
As you're flaming,
That, really, my tears and woes
You care about. Thus fire yearns for
And arrows love
The victory o'er a thousand souls.   36

Ahi devrìa bastar la spoglia
Di mia doglia.
Lumi chiari, lumi rei
I trofei di tanti cori
Sono errori
Da provar gli sdegni miei.   42

Saettar farò mia lira
Piena d'ira
Crudi versi, e'n crudi modi
Vostre frodi altrui diranno,
E faranno
Chiare l'empie vostre lodi.   48

Ma se 'n premio del mio duolo
In me solo
V'affisate. nel mio canto
Vostro vanto in dolci tempre
Dirò sempre,
E porròvi al Sole à canto.   54

Anzi pur dirò, che fugge,
Che si strugge
Al bel vostro lume adorno
Pien di scorno il proprio Sole,
E si duole,
Ch'ei men chiaro adduce il giorno.   60

Alas, the plunder of my woe
Must be enough
You shining lights, you wicked lights;
The trophies of so many hearts
Are errors that
Provoke my scornful diatribes.   42

My lyre will fashion arrows though,
Cruel poems filled
With wrath, and in a fashion cruel
They'll tell of your strange frauds,
And clearly will
They sing the praises of your wickedness.   48

But, when my woe began, if you
Had fixed on me
Alone, then in my song your praise
In keys harmonious I should
Forever sing,
And you could be beside the sun.   54

I'll rather say, the sun itself
That flees, that is
Eclipsed by your fair, golden light
Is sated with disdain and grieves
That he leads forth
The day with light less radiant.   60

Madrigale XXXVI

Qualhor candida, e vaga
Sovra quel, che la cinge oscuro manto
Quella man, che sì dolce il cor m'impiaga
Scope Madonna, io del mio duol mi vanto,
E dico. ah non risplende   5
Sì chiara mai nel suo notturno velo
Stella d'amor nel Cielo.
Insidioso intanto
Trà le vedove bende
Contra me novi lacci Amor pur tende.   10

Madrigale LI

Io t'amo, e ti desìo;
Ma sappi, ch'io non t'amo
Crudel, e non ti bramo
Perch'io mi viva amante
Del lusinghiero tuo vago sembiante.   5
Io t'amo perche'n te vive il cor mio;
E viver non poss'io senza'l mio core.
Dunque è desìo di vita,
Ch'à ciò m'invita, e non forza d'Amore.   9

Madrigal 36

Whenever my lady bares
The hand that wounds my heart so sweetly, white
And lovely beyond the one that closes her
Dark mantle, then I boast about my woe
And say: "Ah never does there shine   5
So bright against its mantle of the night
The star of love in Heaven."
Meanwhile, insidious,
Among the widows' kerchiefs,[54]
New snares Love still sets out to capture me.   10

Madrigal 51

I love you and desire you;
But, Cruel one, be aware,
I do not love or yearn for you
Because I live enthralled
By the false promise of your charming face.   5
I love you, for within you my heart lives;
And I can't stay alive without my heart.
It is desire for life, then,
That urges me to this and not Love's power.   9

Madrigale LIII

Amorosa mia Clori
Se ti rimembra un bacio mi donasti
Lungo questo bel Rìo trà questi fiori;
E s'io tacèa giurasti,
Che mille ancor me ne daresti poi.   5
Io'l tacqui, e'l taccio, e s'io no'l fò palese
Bella Ninfa, e cortese
Perche non servi i giuramenti tuoi?
Baciami, che i tuo' baci
Fìen de la lingua mia nodi tenaci.   10

Scherzo VII

Deh girate
Luci amate
Pietosetto quel bel guardo:
Che mi fugge
Che mi strugge;
Onde'n un m'agghiaccio, ed ardo.   6

O pupille,
Che tranquille
Serenate l'aria intorno:
Sarà mai,
Che i be' rai
Faccian lieto un mio sol giorno?   12

Dolce scocchi
Da quegli occhi
Più del Sol vaghi, ed ardenti
Pìo splendore,
Che ristore
Care luci i miei tormenti.   18

Madrigal 53

My Chloris, amorous,
If you recall, you gave me once a kiss,
Along this rivulet, amongst these flowers;
And, if I curbed my tongue,
You swore you'd give me thousands more of them.   5
I've curbed, do curb it; if I've naught revealed,
Fair nymph, and courteous,
So why do you not now fulfill your oath?
Kiss me, let your kisses
Tie my tongue in firm, unyielding knots.   10

Scherzo 7

Mercifully, Ah
Lights beloved,
Bend on me that lovely gaze,
For it flees me
And destroys me;
Whence at once I burn and freeze.   6

O you pupils
That serenely
Make the air around glow bright,
Will your fair rays
Not make joyful
Ever just one day of mine?   12

O sweet darts shot
From those eyes more
Lovely and brighter than the sun,
Holy splendor,
In my torments,
You restore me, O dear lights.   18

Deh fiameggi,
Deh lampeggi
In quel labro un dolce riso;
In quel labro
Di cinabro,
Che m'ha'l cor dal sen diviso.   24

Amorosa
Graziosa
Di rubini colorita
Tocca il vento
D'un'accento
Bocca; ond'esca la mia vita.   30

Se v'aprite,
Se scoprite
Belle rose amate, e care
Vostre perle,
A vederle
Riderà la Terra, e'l Mare.   36

Non si nieghi
A miei prieghi
Per pietà giusta mercede.
(Ahi) languire,
(Ahi) perire
Deve amando tanta fede?   42

Nò, ch'io scerno
Al governo
Di quei chiari honesti lumi
Amor vero;
Per cui spero
Prìa gioir, ch'i' mi consumi.   48

Ah, you're flaming,
Ah, you're flashing—
On that lip a smile most sweet,
On that lip
Of Cinnabar
That exiled from my breast my heart.   24

Thou so amorous,
Thou so gracious,
Colored with the rubies' hue,
Touch the wind with
One word only—
A word, O mouth, that snares my life.   30

If you open
You reveal there,
O dear roses, fair, beloved,
Pearls of yours that
Just beholding
Makes the earth and sea rejoice.   36

Let my prayers not
Be denied then,
For compassion's mercy just.
Ah to languish,
Ah to perish—
Such great faith must loving have?   42

No, because there
At the helm of
Those bright eyes so chaste I spy
True Love steering;
Thus I'm hopeful
I'll rejoice before I waste away.   48

Nò, che dice
La beatrice
Boca, ov'hor le Grazie stanno,
Havrai, taci
Mille baci
Degno premio à tanto affanno.   54

Al Sig. Ottavio Rinuccini
Che Maravigliosa è la forza della Poesia
Canzonetta Morale IX

Ove trà vaghi fior nascosto è l'Angue
Passa Euridice, e'l fuggitivo piede
L'empio col dente venenoso fiede:
E tanto è'l duol, ch'ella ne cade essangue.   4

Tosto, ch'Orfeo l'inaspettata morte
Di lei, ch'amava sì misero intende,
D'angoscia colmo, e di pietà, discende
De l'empia Dite à le dannate porte.   8

Per la negra palude horrida barca
Piena gli appar di lagrimoso stuolo
D'alme infelici, e Nocchier vecchio, e solo,
Che'l pelago infernal securo varca.   12

E latrar con più gole il Can trifronte
Ode, cui fiera tema il petto assale
Visto trà morti huom vivo, à novo male
(Par dica) havrà per mè quei le man pronte.   16

Con maestà terribile discopre
Pluto seder de l'atra Reggia in mezo,
Che torvo mira nel solfureo lezo
Color, che pari hanno le pene à l'opre.   20

"No," that blessèd
Mouth repeats there
Where the Graces have their place,
"Hush, you'll have a
Thousand kisses,
Worthy prize for such great pain."   54

To Mr. Ottavio Rinuccini[55]
How Marvelous is the power of Poetry
Moral Canzonetta 9

Where midst lovely flowers the serpent's hid
Steps Eurydice, and her straying foot
The evil one with tooth envenomed bites,
And great's the sorrow, for she, lifeless, falls.   4

As soon as wretched Orpheus has heard
Of the unlooked for death of her he loved,
With anguish and with pity filled, he goes
Down to the portals damned of wicked Dis.   8

Through the black marsh a horrid barque appears
Filled with the tearful troop of gloomy souls,
And with an aged helmsman, all alone,
Who plies the infernal sea with confidence.   12

He hears the three-faced dog howl through his throats;
Harsh fear of him assails his breast: Among
The dead a living man he saw, and seemed to say:
"To my woe he'll ready those hands for me."   16

Pluto in terrible majesty he spies
Enthroned in the midst of his gloomy realm.
He grimly peers into the sulfurous stench
At those who feel pain equal to their deeds.   20

Hor s'affisa à i Centauri, ed hor le ciglia
Drizza à colei, che và con l'altre Suore
Di nostra humanità filando l'hore,
E tutta mira al fin l'empia famiglia.   24

I negri Spirti de la notte oscura
Stupidi stanno, e saper brama ogn'uno,
E più'l gran Rè di lagrime digiuno
Quel, che l'ardito giovene procura.   28

Poiche i tant'occhi homai del cieco Regno
Vede à sè volti Orfèo, tende le corde
Perche l'acuto al gràve non discorde,
Indi à la poppa manca appoggia il legno.   32

Marita al suon la voce; e'l grave affanno
Rimbomba dolce sì per le latebre
D'abisso, ch'egli trahe da le palpebre
Il pianto à quei, che lagrimar non sanno.   36

In questi muti campi il passo errante
(Disse) novello Alcide a' danni vostri
Non mov'io già, trà questi oscuri chiostri
D'Euridice mi tragge il bel sembiante.   40

Deh s'amaste giamai tartarei Numi,
La sospirata moglie hor mi rendete,
O me pur, ch'io la veggia ancor tenete;
Che potran quì bearmi i suo' bei lumi.   44

Respirar da l'incarco de' tormenti
L'alme, e col molle canto il duro Fato
Ruppe, ed ottenne il caro pegno amato
Mosse à pietà le dispietate genti.   48

Con legge tal, che non si volga à dietro,
Fin ch'al Regno de' vivi ei non arrive.
Se guarda à tergo empio voler prescrive,
Che la Ninfa ritorni al lago tetro.   52

He stares at centaurs now, now turns his gaze
On her who with her other sisters spins
The hours of our humanity and looks
Intently on the wicked family's end.   24

Black spirits of the gloomy night stand round
Blank-minded, and each yearns to understand,
And most the mighty king bereft of tears,
What thing this daring youth is seeking there.   28

Since Orpheus now sees turned upon himself
The many eyes of that blind realm, he tunes his strings
So high ones won't be out of tune with low,
Then against his left-hand breast he leans his lyre.   32

He weds to its sound his voice; his grievous woe,
Rings out so sweetly through the hidden spots
Of the abyss that from the eyelids of
The ones who cannot weep, he draws a tear.   36

"Into these silent fields with halting step
(He said) a new Alcides for your harms
Amidst these cloisters dark I do not come;
No, I'm drawn by Eurydice's fair face   40

"Ah, if you Tartarean spirits ever loved,
O, give me now my sighed-for wife again;
Or keep me here that I may see her still,
For her lovely lights can even bless me here."   44

The souls gain respite from their burdened pangs,
And with sweet song he overcomes hard Fate
And he obtains his dear, beloved pledge;
To pity the pitiless people he has moved—   48

With this one catch, that he must not look back
Until at the realm of the living he arrives.
If he looks back , the impious will ordains,
Then back to the gloomy lake the Nymph must go.   52

Sì del grembo di morte ei trasse fuora
Il suo tesor; ma poi, ch'à dietro volse
Lo sguardo; il Destin crudo à lui lo tolse.
Ahi vero amor non sà patir dimora.   56

Ma se cotanto ò Rinuccini impetra
Musa gentil, quai grazie uscir veggio
Da la famosa tua vergine Clio;
C'hor vince ogn'alma, ed ogni felce spetra?   60

In morte della molto Illust. Sig.
LAURA GUIDICCIONI LUCCHESINI
Canzone IV

Alma, ch'al Ciel salita
In dubbio hai posto il Mondo
Qual fosse in te maggior senno, ò beltade
Porgi, deh porgi aìta
Al mio dolor profondo.
Da quelle ov'hor ti stai sante contrade
Sfavilla per pietade   7
Un chiarissimo raggio;
Sì che del Mondo impuro
Sgombrandomi l'oscuro
Velo, m'apra del Ciel l'alto viaggio;
Onde beàta un giorno
Riveggia il tuo bel crin di stelle adorno.   13

Havrà ben fin la guerra
Alhor de' miei sospiri
S'avverrà, ch'io ritrovi in Ciel quel bene,
Ch'i' perdei (lassa) in terra.
O beàti martiri,
Se l'effetto gentil d'amica spene
Sarà mai, che v'affrene.   20

Thus from the womb of death he drew her forth,
His treasure, but then, when he turned his glance
Behind, cruel destiny from him tore her.
Woe! True love knows not how to bear delay.   56

But if, O Rinuccini, a gentle muse
May beg, what graces do I see
Come forth from your famed Clio, virgin muse,[56]
Who conquers now each soul, each flinty shade?   60

On the death of the very illustrious Mrs.
LAURA GUIDICCIONI LUCCHESINI[57]
Canzone 4

O soul who's to Heaven ascended,
You have left the world in doubt
Which was greater in you, wisdom or loveliness.
Give succor, ah bring me aid in
My sorrow most profound.
From those holy realms where now you dwell,
For pity let a ray   7
Shine forth—one very bright—
So unencumbered by
This impure world's dark veil
The lofty way to Heaven is opened for me
So blest I shall one day
Look on your star-crowned, lovely locks again.   13

The war then of my sighs
Will surely end, and it
Will come to pass that I'll refind in Heaven
That good I lost (alas) on earth.
O, if ever, blessèd pains,
The noble result of heartening hope was that
You were restrained by it.   20

Chiudami gli occhi Morte,
S'aprir mi deve il Fato
L'almo sentier beàto,
Ch'altrui conduce à la superna Corte.
Hor giunga il fin di questa
Vita, se tal principio à me s'appresta.   26

O Laura mia quel Lauro,
Da cui prendesti il nome,
C'hebbe già da tuoi versi honor cotanto
Qual havrà più restauro?
Perch'ei cinga le chiome
Di Poeti, e d'Heroi non si dia vanto,
Che la porpora, e'l canto,   33
E di quelli, e di questi
Quella gloria gli dia,
Che già tù Laura mia
Col nome, e con la cetra aurea gli desti.
Ecco ei già langue, e perde
Da te lontano, e le sue frondi, e'l verde.   39

Il tuo diletto Sposo
Anch'ei perduto hà (lasso)
Di sua vita mortal l'hore tranquille.
Al ciglio lagrimoso
Sembra un'immobil sasso,
Che duo Fonti di lagrime distille;
Nè però le faville,   46
Che'n se racchiude il petto
Scemar ponno l'ardore;
Che quando altri nel core
Porta di casto foco honesto affetto
Vive l'incendio, e dura
Quand'ancor chi l'accese è terra oscura.   52

Let Death now close my eyes,
If Fate ordains for me
The blest, life-giving path
Be opened that led her to the court divine.
Let this life's end come now
If such a beginning lies in store for me.   26

O Laura mine, will that
Laurel whence you took your name,
That from your verse such honor already had,
Ever again revive?
Because it crowns the locks
Of poets and heroes, it should not boast of that,
For the purple and the song,   33
Of those as well as these,
Will give to them that glory
Which you already with
Your name, my Laura, and
Your golden lyre as well has given them.
Lo, far from you, that Laurel wilts
Indeed; it sheds its leaves—its green is gone.   39

Your loving husband too
Has also lost (alas)
The tranquil hours of his mortal life.
His tearful brow appears
To be a rigid stone
From which two weeping founts are gushing forth.
Yet those tears cannot ease   46
The burning sparks that he
Conceals within his breast;
For when one bears within
His heart chaste love's unsullied fire, the flame
Endures and lives though she
Who kindled it has turned to gloomy earth.   52

Sovente lagrimando
La sua sventura ei dice,
Cara del viver mio fida compagna
Lasso me, lasso quando
Sarò teco felice,
E di lagrime pure il volto bagna.
Così s'afflige, e lagna;   59
E viè più cresce il duolo,
Perche'n angosce tante
Non hà'l misero amante
Per temprar tanti affanni un piacer solo;
Ed estrema è la doglia,
Che di speme, e conforto empia ne spoglia.   65

E chi può nel confine
Frenar de la ragione
Alma beàta, che dal Ciel m'ascolti
Un dolor senza fine?
Ne l'angusta prigione
Del cor son troppi danni insieme accolti.
A lagrimar son volti   72
Homai tutti i mortali;
Ma ben che un largo fonte
Versi ogn'huom da la fronte
Le lagrime non vanno al duolo eguali;
Nè basta humano accento
A sfogar quest'interno aspro tormento.   78

Qui chiuso posa ò Viator gentile
Di LAURA il nobil velo
Sparsa in terra è la fama, e l'Alma è'n Cielo.   81

He, frequently in tears,
Of his misfortune speaks:
"My faithful consort, dear one of my life,
Ah woe, alas, with you
When shall I happy be?"
And with pure tears he bathes his countenance.
He grieves thus and laments—   59
Makes sorrow grow the more,
For in such anguish drear
The wretched lover has
No single joy to temper such great pain;
His sorrow is extreme,
His grief strips him of comfort and of hope.   65

And who can, in the grip
Of sorrow without end,
Be ruled by reason, O blessed soul who hears
Me from the Heavens?
In the strait prison of
His heart too many harms have thronged at once.
Thenceforth to weeping have   72
All mortals turned; but though
An ample spring flows from
Each person's brow, the tears
Aren't equal to the sorrow's pangs,
For human words do not
Suffice to vent this inner torment harsh.   78

Here, O gentle traveler, lies enclosed
Our LAURA's noble veil;
Through earth her fame is spread; her soul's in Heaven.   81

Nel medesimo soggetto

Sonetto CVIII

Quanti trofèi già d'arme vaga, e quanti
Guerrier togliesti à noi d'alto valore
O Morte? e quanti al bel Regno d'Amore
Fiera involasti pellegrini Amanti?   4

Talhor gemme predasti, e regi manti,
Incendesti Città vaga d'ardore,
Bramosa poi di lagrimoso humore
Di mille occhi bevesti i larghi pianti;   8

Chi la strage, c'hai fatta di beltade
Sperando d'abbellirti dir potrebbe,
E de i cari à le Muse illustri ingegni?   11

E vaga pur di fregi alteri, e degni
Un Lauro hai svelto à questa nostra etade,
Che Tessaglia, nè Sorga un tal non hebbe.   14

Nell'istessa occasione

Madrigale LV

Trà questi duri sassi
Laura, che tanto amai
Laura mia, ch'amo ancor rinchiusa stassi.
Tù Viator, che passi
Quì le più degne Dee veder potrai,   5
Che tutte insieme accolte
Piangono l'honorate ossa sepolte.
Sol la diva beltà mirar non puoi,
Che seco Laura mia la tolse à noi.   9

On the same subject
(the death of Laura Guidiccioni Lucchesini)
Sonnet 108

How many trophies of splendid arms, O Death,
How many warriors high in our esteem
Have you seized? How many pilgrim lovers bound
For Love's fair realm, O fierce one, have you snatched?　　4

Sometimes you've pillaged gems, and royal cloaks,
You've burned a lovely town with raging heat,
Then, thirsting for the tearful humor, you
Have drunk of a thousand eyes the welling tears.　　8

Who could describe the slaughter you have wrought,
Hoping with beauty to adorn yourself—
And with the Muses' darlings' glorious gifts.　　11

And fancying just such high and worthy traits,
A laurel you've uprooted in our time
That neither Thessaly nor Sorgue could match.[58]　　14

On the same occasion
(the death of Laura Guidiccioni Lucchesini)
Madrigal 55

Among these stones so hard,
Laura whom I loved so much—
Still love—O Laura mine, you lie enclosed.
You, passing traveler,
Can see the goddesses most worthy here,　　5
For gathered all they mourn the honored bones
Entombed. You just can't see the loveliness
Divine that with her my Laura took from us.　　9

Centone I. Tutto de' versi del Petrarca

Chi pensò mai veder fra terra oscura
Due rose fresche, e colte in Paradiso,
Che dal Mondo m'havean tutto diviso
Dolcemente obliando ogn'altra cura?   4

Qualhor veggio cangiata sua figura,
E'l lampeggiar de l'angelico riso
Piovommi amare lagrime dal viso.
Ahi null'altro, che pianto al Mondo dura.   8

Quella, che fù mia Donna al Cielo è gita
Tal fù mia stella, e tal mia cruda sorte
Per far me stesso à me più grave salma.   11

A l'ultimo bisogno ò miser'Alma
E l'aura mia vital da me partita;
Nè contra Morte spero altro, che Morte.   14

Madrigale 77

O Mia Nisa, ò mio cor mentr'io vagheggio
Quelle tue belle chiome,
E que' begli occhi, io veggio,   3
Io veggio in quelle il Sole, in questi Amore.
Che l'un (ne sò ben come)
M'infiamma, e l'altro mi saetta il core.   6

Cento 1. All from Petrarch's lines
(On the death of Laura Guidiccioni Lucchesini)

Whoever thought to see become dark earth[59]
Two roses freshly picked in Paradise[60]
That from the world had wholly carried me,[61]
Forgetting sweetly every other care?[62]   4

At those times that I see her shape transformed,[63]
And her angelic smile like lightning flash,[64]
My bitter tears fall raining from my face.[65]
Woe! Nothing, save for tears, in this world lasts.[66]   8

That one who was my lady passed to heaven,[67]
My star was such, and such my bitter lot[68]
To make me a great burden to myself.[69]   11

In this last need of yours, O wretched soul,[70]
That gentle breeze that gave me life left me;[71]
To counter Death, I hope for naught but Death.[72]   14

Madrigal 77

O Nisa mine, O my heart, when I gaze
With love upon your lovely locks,
And on those lovely eyes, I see—   3
I see in those the Sun and Love in these.
For the one (I know not how)
Inflames me, and the other wounds my heart.   6

Madrigale LXXX

Per pietà di me stesso
Me medesmo bandisco
Da quel bel volto, c'ho ne l'alma impresso,   3
Perche qualhor ardisco
D'avvicinarmi à quei duo soli ardenti
Provo per un piacer mille tormenti.   6

Madrigale LXXXIII

Porta la Donna mia
Al bel collo sospeso
Vagò ornamento, che le addìta l'hore;
Industre, e ricco sì, ma inutil peso.
S'ella non hà pietà del mio dolore,   5
S'ella il mio duol non crede
A che misura'l tempo? hor non s'avede,
Che mentr'ella mi sprezza
Fugge con l'hore ancor la sua bellezza?   9

Madrigale XC

In leggiadretta gonna,
Che d'azurro, e d'argento intessut'era
Ella m'apparve, ch'è del mio cor Donna,
E ben sembrommi alhor senz'alcun velo
Veder Cinthia nel Cielo;   5
Indi à gli occhi s'offerse in vesta nera;
E d'Amor Maga vera
Sparse tenebre, e luce d'ogn'intorno;
Che la notte ci addusse il fosco manto,
E'l viso honesto, e santo il chiaro giorno.   10

Madrigal 80

In pity for myself,
Myself I'm banishing
From that fair face emblazoned on my soul;   3
For when I've courage to
Approach that lovely pair of burning suns,
To try one joy I bear a thousand pangs.   6

Madrigal 83

A charming ornament
Around her lovely neck
My lady wears that counts the hours for her;
A busy, rich, but, really, useless weight.
If she won't have pity on my sorrow,   5
If she won't give credit to my woe,
Why measure time? Does she not now perceive
That while she's snubbing me
Her beauty with the hours flees away?   9

Madrigal 90

In a captivating gown
With silver interwoven and with blue
The lady of my heart appeared to me,
And indeed I seemed to see unveiled
In heaven Cynthia herself;   5
Next, dressed in black, she stood before my eyes;
Love's true enchantress, she
Was scattering light and shadow everywhere;
Her dark cloak led the night to us,
Her chaste and holy face brought shining day.   10

Chapter 2

Scherzo VIII

Con quai giri lascivetti
Hoggi alletti
Zefiretto la mia Clori?
Del suo bel ti vai pascendo
(Ahi) fingendo
Rasciugarle i bei sudori.   6

Tù scherzando hor fuggi, hor riedi,
Hor ti siedi
Lievemente in quel bel petto;
Hor increspi i capei biondi,
Hor t'ascondi
Entro'l labbro amorosetto.   12

Con quant'arte l'aure molci,
Come dolci
Movi, e freschi i tuoi sospiri;
Come in tanto lusingando
Vai predando
Quel odor, che grato spiri.   18

Non però le rose, e i gigli,
Onde pigli
Le tue grazie perdon mai
Il tesor, che stassi accolto
In quel volto,
Ch'è del Sol più chiaro assai.   24

O trè volte, e più felice
Tè, cui lice
Vagheggiar l'almo sembiante,
E baciarlo, mentre in vano
Quasi insano
Verso (ohime) lagrime tante.   30

Scherzo 8

With what engaging swirlings
Do you charm my
Chloris, gentle Zephyr—sprite, today?
You graze upon her beauty while
(Ah, me!) you feign
To dry her perspiration sweet.   6

Now playfully you flee, now laugh,
Now sprightly you
Alight upon that lovely breast,
Now twirl those tresses blond,
Now hide yourself
Within that tempting lip.   12

How deftly breezes you caress,
How sweet and cool
The sighs you quicken; how, too,
With flattering deceit you wend
While plundering
That pleasant fragrance you breathe forth.   18

The roses and the lilies, though,
From which you glean
Such graces, do not ever lose
Their treasure, for it was stored
In that face which
Shines so much brighter than the sun.   24

O you, thrice over happiest,
Who's privileged
Lovingly to gaze upon
Her countenance
Sublime and kiss it, while in vain
Almost insane
I shed (alas) so many tears.   30

Freddo spirto (ah) sì beato
Nel tuo stato
Senza gielo non saresti,
Che sarian que' rai lucenti
Sì possenti,
Che d'amor meco arderesti.   36

Madrigale XCIX

Ove sì tosto voli
Sogno? deh non partire,
Poiche dolce consoli
L'amaro, ed angoscioso mio martire.
Se pietosa tù sol Madonna fai   5
Del mio lungo languire
Cortese ingannator, perche te n' vai?
Ben è ver, che'l contento
D'Amor fugge qual nube innanzi al vento.   9

Madrigale CII

De la mia bella Donna
Un dì vestì la gonna Amore; ed ella
Prese d'Amor, e l'arco, e le quadrella;
E chiunque vedèa
L'uno, e l'altra credèa,   5
Ch'Amor fosse mia Donna, e fosse Amore
La mia leggiadra Dèa.
Ma chi scerner potrìa sì dolce errore,
S'Amor, e questa mia possente Maga
Egualmente n'impiaga?   10

Cold spirit, ah! so blessèd
For in your state
You'll never be without your chill;
Because so potent are those lucent rays
They'd make you burn
Along with me because of love.   36

Madrigal 99

Where so quickly do you fly,
O dream? Ah, do not go away because
You bring sweet comfort to
My bitter and my anguished suffering.
If you alone can make my lady merciful   5
Toward my long languishing,
O courteous trickster, why do you go away?
It's true indeed: the happiness
Of Love flees like a cloud before the wind.   9

Madrigal 102

One day Love donned the gown
My lovely lady wore; and both Love's bow
And his four-sided darts she took from him;
And whosoever looked upon
The one, and on the other thought   5
My lady to be Love and Love to be
My captivating goddess.
But who such a sweet error could discern
If Love, and this enchantress powerful
Of mine can wound me equally?   10

Madrigale CIII

Languisco, e son tant'anni
Cruda mia Tigre, e voi
Non date fede a' miei sì lunghi affanni.
Mi crederete poi,   4
Ch'io sarò giunto à morte,
Ed havrete pietà de la mia sorte;
Ma 'ntempestiva giunge
Pietà, se tardi un duro petto punge.   8

Madrigale CIV

Donna se voi poteste
Veder il mio martir, sicome io veggio
L'infinita beltà, che'n voi risplende:
Forse quando pietade humil vi chieggio,
Che'l vostro orgoglio al mio desir contende: 5
Vi mostrereste pìa;
Ma perche eterna la mia doglia sia
Quanto più veggio la bellezza vostra
Tanto meno il mio vale à voi si mostra.   9

Scherzo IX

Moveà dolce un zefiretto
I suoi tepidi sospiri:
E lasciando l'aureo letto
Fiammeggiò per gli alti giri
L'Alba; e'l Mondo colorìo
Mentre rose, e gigli aprìo.   6

Madrigal 103

I languish, and have done
Long years, my tiger fierce,
But in my grief so long you don't believe.
You will believe me when   4
I shall have met my death
And you regret my fate;
Untimely pity comes, though,
If late it penetrates a stony breast.   8

Madrigal 104

If, Lady, you were able
To see my suffering the way I see
The beauty infinite that shines in you,
Perhaps when, humble, mercy I entreat
From you, since your pride vies with my desire,   5
You would show clemency.
But since my sorrow will forever last,
The more I gaze upon your loveliness,
The less my worth to you appears to be.   9

Scherzo 9

A gentle breeze was breathing softly
Its warm sighs, and rising from
Her golden bed the Dawn flamed forth
Throughout the lofty circles of the spheres;
And she brought color to the world
While roses opened and the lilies too.   6

Quando Ninfa Amor m'offerse,
Ch'adornò d'altr'Alba i campi.
Forse Pari in Ida scerse
Così chiari ardenti lampi.
Nò, che Venere si crede
Finta alhor, che costei vede.   12

Ella ornava gli ornamenti
Col sembiante pellegrino;
E gioivan gli elementi
Vagheggiando il bel divino;
E sù l'oro de i capelli
Rideàn lieti i fior novelli.   18

Febo uscì de l'onde fuore;
Ma poi ch'egli in terra scorse
D'altri raggi altro splendore
Saggio indietro il camin torse.
Che s'ei fosse in Ciel comparso
Fora stato e vinto, ed arso.   24
Le fresch'aure matutine

S'infiammàro al dolce foco
De le labbra porporine;
De le labbra, ov'hoggi han loco
Di rubin vive facelle,
Ch'ardon l'alme, ardon le stelle.   30

Il bel petto ove biancheggia
Di sue nevi il giglio pieno
Che mille occhi il Ciel vagheggia;
Nè sò ancor se'n quel bel seno
Scendon guardi, ò scendon baci
Del mio ben ladri rapaci.   36

'Twas then Love offered me a nymph
Who with a second Dawn adorned the fields.
Maybe there in Ida Paris[73]
Viewed such bright and shining eyes.
(No, for it's believed he saw
A simulated Venus in that place.)   12

She was gracing all that beauty
With a pilgrim's countenance;
And on her loveliness divine,
The elements rejoiced to gaze;
And atop her golden tresses
Joyfully rare flowers laughed.   18

From the waves had Phoebus risen,
But when on the earth he saw
From other rays another splendor,
Wisely back his chariot he turned.
Had he in the sky contended,
Scorched and conquered, he'd have been cast out.   24

The cool breezes of the morning
Warmed themselves at the sweet flame
Of her lips vermilion hued,
Of her lips where sparks from rubies
Have their dwelling place today—
Sparks that kindle souls, light up the stars.   30

On that fair breast, whence the lily
Filled the whiteness of its snows,
With a thousand eyes the heavens gazed.
I don't know if on that lovely breast
Those gazes rest still or if kisses drop—
Thieves rapacious of my own well-being.   36

Pure nevi, che accendete
Le faville, ond'io tutt'ardo
Morte voi, voi tomba sete
Del famelico mio sguardo,
Del mio sguardo, che Fenice
Nel morir divien felice.   42

Dolci pomi, ed acerbetti
Pur quel candido sentiero
Veggio in voi, ch'almi diletti
Mi promette; per voi spero
Che trà neve, e neve ardendo
Vada l'alma al Ciel salendo.   48

Ma perch'altri, ov'io non poggi
A me solo Amor gentile
Scopri i duo nevosi poggi,
Che fiorir fan vago Aprile;
Che lampeggian fiamme d'oro;
A tè gloria, à me tesoro.   54

O se tanto mi concedi
Amor, vedi, nel mio canto
Dirà Clio tuo nobil vanto.   57

Pure white snows, these sparks you kindle
By which I'm entirely burned,
You're the death, the tomb as well
Of my gaze so ravenous,
Of my gaze because the Phoenix
Finds, in dying, happiness.   42

Apples sweet and slightly tart too,
In you I can surely see
That shining pathway, for you promise
Vivifying joys to me;
Through you I hope that, all aflame,
From snow to snow my soul to heaven may rise.   48

But, since I may not elsewhere rest,
To me alone will kindly Love
Reveal that pair of snowy hillocks
That make sweet April burst with bloom;
That set alight the golden flames,
For you, glory; for me, treasure.   54

O Love, if so much you will grant me,
In this song of mine you'll see
Clio speaking forth your noble praise.[74]   57

Sonetto CLIII

Anima stanca à che sospiri, e piagni?
È sordo à' tuoi sospir, cieco al tuo pianto
Quei per cui notte, e dì ti struggi, e lagni,
Quei, che l'angosce tue si prende à vanto.   4

Ahi se lunge da lui sol' godo quanto
Mi son pianti, e sospir fidi compagni
Perche vuoi, che da loro io mi scompagni?
Doppia il duol de gli afflitti il riso, e'l canto.   8

Sfogo così del tormentoso petto
L'aspro martir, che sol s'alleggia, e molce
Al chiaro lume de l'amato oggetto.   11

Trabocchi in pianto pur l'interno affetto.
Non è forse talhora il pianger dolce?
Han le lagrime anch'esse il lor diletto.   14

Madrigale CXII

È Spento il foco, è spento,
Ond'io vissi piangendo
Lassa non men che ardendo.   3
Nè sia, ch'io senta più d'amor tormento
Se di novo Prometeo non riforma
Del cener tuo la tua leggiadra forma.   6

Sonnet 153

For whom do you sigh and weep, O weary soul?
Deaf to your sighs is that one, blind to tears—
Those that ravage and tear you night and day,
Those that your griefs can take the credit for.   4

Oh, if away from him I just enjoy
Such steadfast companions as my tears and sighs,
Why do you want me to send them away from me?
Sorrow strips song and laughter from the grieved.   8

Thus do I vent from my tortured breast the harsh
Distress that only in the shining light
Of what one loves will take cheer and be eased.   11

Even my inner feelings brim with tears.
Isn't weeping sometimes sweet, perhaps?
Tears also bring a pleasure of their own.   14

Madrigal 112

The fire's burnt out, burnt out,
For which I once lived weeping
No less, alas, than burning,   3
Nor will I feel love's torment any more
Unless Prometheus again reforms
From your ashes your charming shape again.[75]   6

Madrigale CXVII

Standomi dietro ad una quercia antica
Vidi in un chiaro fonte
Le bianche mani, e la serena fronte
Bagnarsi à l'empia mia dolce nemica,
Poi fuggirsene al monte.   5
Io (lasso) al fonte corsi,
E l'onda amata bebbi, e non m'accorsi,
Ch'ella accesa n'havèa l'onda gelata;
Tal, ch'io ne porto piú l'alma infiammata.   9

Madrigale CXXII

Quella bocca di rose
La mia vaga Licori
Tutta ridente, e bella
In premio al fin de' miei gravi dolori   4
Mi porge lieta. (ahi scaltra Pastorella)
Ecco i' la bacio, ed ella,
Che'n bocca asconde l'amorose Faci
M'incende l'alma co' suoi dolci baci.   8

Madrigale CXXIII

Per fuggir la prigione,
Il giogo, e la catena, ov'io tant'anni
Vissi tiranneggiata in tanti affanni,
Per compagna Ragione,   4
Per consiglier lo Sdegno, Ira per guida
Prendo così l'infida
Fede io fuggo d'Amor, le reti, e i dardi;
Ma lassa (ohime,) ch'io me n'avveggio tardi.   8

Madrigal 117

Standing behind an ancient oak tree once
I saw in a clear fount
The white hands being bathed and the clear brow
Of my sweet, wicked enemy, who then
From there to the mountains fled.   5
I ran to the fount, alas,
And drank the beloved waters, did not note
That she had set aflame the icy waves;
I suffer from that a soul yet more inflamed.   9

Madrigal 122

That mouth of roses,
Lovely liquor mine
All smiling, beautiful,
As a reward at last for my grave woes   4
She offers, glad (ah, cunning shepherdess!).
I kiss her, lo, and she
Who in her mouth hides amorous jests
With her sweet kisses sets my soul aflame.   8

Madrigal 123

To flee the prison, flee
The yoke and chains where I for many years
Lived tyrannized in many sufferings,
As a companion I   4
Took Reason, took Disdain as counselor,
Wrath for a guide, and thus
Love's faithless faith I flee, his snares and darts;
But woe (alas!) that late I heeded them.   8

Sonetto CLIX

Con lagrime di sangue, e con sospiri
Di foco trassi la mia stanca vita
Per aspro calle un tempo; e'nvano aita,
Invan chiesi pietà de' miei martiri.   4

Pur si cangiàro al fin gli empi desiri
Del cor nemici, e la mortal ferita
Saldò Ragione; ond'hor veggio pentita
Gli andati errori ovunque gli occhi i' giri.   8

Saggia hor seguo il mio ben, poich'io ti fuggo
Mostro infernal; son di me stessa amica
Fatta nemica al tuo spietato inganno.   11

Hor non vivo morendo, hor non mi struggo,
Nel gielo altrui: spenta è la fiamma antica;
E me stess'amo hor, ch'odio Amor tiranno.   14

Sonnet 159

One time I used to drag my weary life
Along rough paths with tears of blood and sighs
Of fire; and all help was in vain—in vain
The pity I begged for all my sufferings.   4

Though in the end the wicked wishes of
My heart—its foes—were changed, and Reason healed
The mortal wound; whence every place I turn
My eyes I see the errors passing penitent.   8

Now wisely my best interests I pursue
Because, infernal monster, I flee you;
I'm my own friend, foe to your spiteful fraud.   11

I do not now live dying, or destroy
Myself in someone's ice; the old flame's out;[76]
I love myself, for I hate the tyrant Love.   14

In morte del Sig. Torquato Tasso
Sonetto CLXIX

Hor qual grave per l'aria odo lamento?
Ond'è, che rugiadoso ognun il ciglio
Danna di Morte il dispietato artiglio,
C'have d'Apollo il maggior lume spento?   4

La nostra gloria, il gran TORQUATO io sento
Gridar miseri è morto; è morto il figlio
De l'alte Muse, onde l'amaro essiglio
Ogni nostro piacer volge in tormento.   8

Chi la mente v'accieca egri mortali.
Morir può quei, che col suo divo ingegno
Rese à l'Eternità mill'altri eguali?   11

Saggio il TASSO aspirando al santo Regno
Spiegò celeste Cigno altero l'ali
Lasciando il Mondo di sua luce indegno.   14

On the Death of Mr. Torquato Tasso[77]
Sonnet 169

What grave dirge am I hearing in the air?
Whence comes it that (this moistens every lash)
All curse the unpitying claws of Death,
That has put out Apollo's brightest light?   4

"Our glory, the great TORQUATO's dead," I hear
The cry; "Oh wretched, the lofty Muses' son
Is dead whose bitter exile turns
Our every pleasure into suffering."   8

Who blinds your minds, O mortals frail?
Can someone die who with his godlike skill
Shapes for the ages a thousand like himself?   11

Wise TASSO, aiming toward the holy realm,
A celestial swan, he spread his lofty wings,[78]
Leaving a world unworthy of his light.   14

Del Sig. Gabriello Chiabrera
Sonetto CLXXI

Nel giorno, che sublime in bassi manti
Isabella imitava alto furore;
E stolta con angelici sembianti
Hebbe del senno altrui gloria maggiore;   4

Alhor saggia tra'l suon, saggia trà i canti.
Non mosse piè, che non scorgesse Amore,
Nè voce aprì, che non creasse amanti,
Nè riso fè, che non beasse un core.   8

Chi fù quel giorno à rimirar felice
Di tutt'altro quà gîù cesse il desìo,
Che sua vita per sempre hebbe serena.   11

O di Scena dolcissima Sirena,
O de' Teatri Italici Fenice,
O trà Coturni insuperabil Clìo.   14

By Mr. Gabriello Chiabrera
Sonnet 171

Upon that day, sublime in humble garb,
Isabella performed with inspiration high
And, foolish with an angel's countenance,
Greater glory over others' minds she won.   4

Wise then amidst the music, shrewd midst songs,
She took no step that Love did not direct,
Uttered no word but made some lover love,
And smiled no smile that did not bless some heart.   8

Whoever watched upon that happy day
Ceased wanting all things else upon the earth
Because his life forever grew serene.   11

O sweetest Siren of the scene and stage,
O Phoenix of Italian Theaters,
O Clio, treading on the peerless boards.[79]   14

Risposta
Sonetto CLXXII

La tua gran Musa hor che non può? quand'ella
Mè stolta fà de l'altrui senno altera
Vittrice; ond'è, ch'ogni più dotta schiera
Furor insano alto saver appella.   4

Queste mie spoglie, il canto, la favella,
Il riso, e'l moto spiran grazie; e vera
Fatta (pur sua mercè) d'Amor guerriera
Avento mille à i cor faci, e quadrella.   8

Ma s'ella tanto con lo stile adorno
Hà forza; in me col suo valor accenda
Foco; onde gloria ne sfavilli intorno.   11

Per lei mio carme à nobil fama ascenda
CHIABRERA illustre; ed avverrà, che un giorno
Degno cambio di rime anch'io ti renda.   14

Response
Sonnet 172
(Andreini's reply to Chiabrera)

What now can your great Muse not do? When she
Makes foolish me the victress over the
High sense of others; so each more learned troop
Calls demented furor "wisdom high"?   4

The graces inspire these shifts of mine, the song,
The motion, the speech, the smile; yes, thanks to Love,
I'm made Love's warrior, in truth, Love's lance,
Flung into hearts inflamed a thousand times.   8

But if she, so much enriched with style,
Has strength; let him with his valor in me
Strike fire whose glory may around us glow.   11

For you may my poem rise to noble fame
Illustrious CHIABRERA; and one day let
Me give you back a worthy exchange in rhyme.   14

Sonetto CLXXXV

Se per quelli salvar, ch'errar vedesti,
Se per campargli da l'eterna morte
Senza partir da la celeste Corte
Signor per tua pietà frà noi scendesti;   4

Quel sangue prezioso, che spargesti
Tragga me da le vie fallaci, e torte;
E mi richiami à più felice sorte,
Anzi che di mia vita il fin s'appresti.   8

E come da gli altrui devoti preghi
Mosso, chiamasti del sepolcro fuori
O gran Figlio di Dio Lazaro estinto.   11

Così la tua pietade hoggi non nieghi
Di chiamar lo mio cor per morte vinto
Da la Tomba infelice de gli errori.   14

Sonnet 185[80]

Just to save the ones whom you saw err,
Just from eternal death to rescue them,
Without departing the celestial court,
You, Lord, for pity, in our midst came down.   4

May that precious blood you shed draw me away
From twisted byways and the wrongful path
And call me to a happier port again,
Indeed my life is coming near its end.   8

And just as you were moved by others' prayers
Devout to do, you called forth from the tomb
Dead Lazarus, O mighty Son of God.   11

So in your pity, don't refuse today
To call my heart, by you through death redeemed,
From the unhappy sepulchre of sin.   14

Sonetto CLXXXVI

Hor che strale d'Amor più non m'offende;
Ne'l suo velen di dolce amaro infetto
Scorre per l'ossa; e per terreno oggetto
La sua fiamma infernal più non m'incende;   4

Quel Sol, ch'eterno trà beàti splende
M'allumi; e dolce mi riscaldi il petto,
Sì, ch'arda sol' in me quel puro affetto,
Che da' raggi purissimi discende.   8

Deh se priego mortal tant'alto arriva
Opra dolce Signor, che l'alma mia
Seguendo il tuo d'ogn'altro amor sia schiva.   11

Purghi'l suo error tua fiamma e santa, e pia;
Onde fatta serena in tè sol viva.
Pur tua pietade altrui falli oblìa.   14

Sonnet 186

Now that Love's arrows do me no more harm—
Nor does his tainted poison, bittersweet,
Run through my bones—nor his infernal flame
More kindle me with any earthly thing,   4

May that Sun, which always shines amidst the blest,
Illumine me and sweetly warm my breast,
So that in me pure love alone may shine
That takes its origin from purest rays.   8

Ah, if a mortal prayer can reach so high,
Sweet Lord, so order it that my soul shuns
All other love by following yours alone.   11

Let your holy, righteous flame purge my soul's sin;
Serene, thus, I shall live in you alone,
For your mercy obliterates a person's faults.   14

Sonetto CXCIV

Sgombra, sgombra da te mio tristo core
Le 'ndegnissime tue fiamme cocenti,
Ardito scaccia homai cure, e tormenti,
Onde t'afflige il tuo nemico Amore.   4

Sfavilla Anima mia del puro ardore
Di chi formò le stelle, e gli elementi,
Porgi le orecchie à suoi divini accenti,
Lava del tuo fallir l'antico errore.   8

Troverai se ti penti in Ciel pietade;
Che gravi sì le colpe tue non sono,
Che viè maggior non sia l'alta clemenza.   11

Sì di Ninive già l'empia cittade
Venuta del suo fallo à penitenza
Hebbe del suo fallir grato perdono.   14

Sonnet 194

Sweep clean, sweep clean from yourself, my sorrowful heart,
Those most unworthy, searing flames of yours,
Boldly banish henceforth the torments, cares,
With which your foeman Love distresses you. 4

Shine forth my soul with the ardor pure of him
Who formed the stars and shaped the elements,
Attune your ears to his accents divine;
The ancient error of your faults wash clean. 8

If you repent, you'll mercy find in Heaven;
For your transgressions aren't so very grave
That there's not greater lofty clemency. 11

So with Nineveh, a wicked town indeed,
When for its fault it came to penitence,
It received a welcome pardon for its sin.[81] 14

Sonetto CXCV

Io vissi un tempo (ond'hor meco mi sdegno)
Tiranneggiata da mortal desiro,
E soffersi infelice il giogo indegno
Di strano, e di gravissimo martiro;   4

E sì fui priva de l'usato ingegno,
Che'l proprio error non vidi; aperto hor miro
D'Amor tiranno il micidial disegno,
E di Fortuna il sempre instabil giro.   8

Hor che (la Dio mercè) pur veggio fuora
Quest'alma de l'antico, e cieco errore
Veggio anco il fosco de' gran falli suoi.   11

Tal nulla vede il Peregrin qualhora
Di nebbia è cinto; e'l tutto scorge poi,
Ch'ei lascià dietro il tenebroso horrore.   14

Madrigale CXXV

Qual candida Colomba
Il suo pennuto manto
Terge lieta, e vagheggia,
E poi festosa al Ciel dispiega i vanni.
Tal io vissuta in pianto   5
Colpa d'Amor molt'anni
Già tratto'l piè da la sua 'ngiusta Reggia
In questo Fonte santo
Di pentimento purgo il fallir mio,
E lieta al Ciel le mie speranze invìo.   10

Sonnet 195

I lived once (whence I now disdain myself)
Tyrannized by mortal longing, and I,
Unhappy, suffered the unworthy yoke
Of torment strange and very burdensome.   4

And I was so bereft of normal wit
That my own sin I saw not; clearly now
I see the deadly plan of tyrant Love,
And Fortune's ever unstable whirl I watch.   8

Now that (thank God!) this soul I see indeed
Beyond that old blind error, I can see
As well the gloom of its great faults.   11

So sometimes when a pilgrim's cloaked in mist,
He nothing sees, and then sees everything
When the dark horror he has left behind.   14

Madrigal 125

Just as a pure white dove
Its feathered mantle preens
In joy and with delight,
And then for heaven merrily spreads its wings,
So I who'd lived in tears   5
Love-struck—after long years
I dragged my feet from his unjust domain—
In this Font sanctified
I washed transgression clean with penitence,
And joyfully my hope toward heaven I send.   10

Incantesimo egloga III
Argomento

Una Ninfa innamorata fieramente di Tirsi Pastore apparate alcune cose
da maga Donna, per mezo di quelle si studia richiamarlo al suo primo
amore, dal quale ei s'era tolto, e vedendole riuscir vane, le danna,
risolvendosi di non creder mai più alle loro bugie.

Hor che la Notte à la suprema altezza
Giunta del Ciel verso l'Hibero fugge;
Hor, che sopite in un soàve oblìo
Tien le fatiche de' mortali il sonno;
Hor che taccion le frondi   5
Al tranquillo tacer de le mort'aure,
Nè de la Terra il duro volto preme
Col passo errante, ò fiera,
Od huom, che tutto è dal silenzio oppresso;
E quei dorme securo   10
In grotta alpina, e questi
In pagliaresco albergo
Posando, i lumi chiude.
Io fatta già da l'empio Armor tiranno
Di Ninfa belva, à l'aria humida, e fosca   15
M'accingo à richiamar Tirsi crudele
Con magiche parole,
E con herbe recise al Sol notturno:
Tirsi crudel, ch'à l'amor mio s'è tolto.

Spargi Clori il terren de l'acque, ch'io   20
Tolsi da tre Fontane; e'l novo Altare
Fatto di terra, e d'herbe intorno cingi
Tre volte, e quattro con le molli bende;
Poi la casta verbena, e'l maschio incenso
Accendi; e'n bassa voce   25

Sorcery, Eclogue 3
Argument

A nymph, wildly enamored of the shepherd Thyrsis, acquired from a lady sorceress some paraphernalia by means of which she endeavors to recall him to his first love, from whom he had been drawn away, and finding vain success in them, she curses them, resolving never more to believe in their lies.

[The Nymph Chloris speaks:]
"Now when, once having reached its highest point,
Night takes its flight toward winter from the sky;
Now when, lulled into sweet forgetfulness,
These mortal beings' labors Sleep suspends;
Now that fronds keep silence at   5
The tranquil silence of the dead-still breeze,
And there's no man or beast to press upon
The hard-faced earth their footprints wandering,
When everything's with silence battened down,
And some are sleeping safe   10
In Alpine grottos, some
In rustic huts repose,
Their eyelids tightly closed,
I, surely forced by Love malevolent,
A tyrant o'er a woodland nymph, set out   15
In damp, dark air to reclaim Thyrsis cruel
With magic hexes and
With herbs I gathered under nighttime sun:[82]
Cruel Thyrsis, who's defected from my love."

[The sorceress speaks:]
"Sprinkle, O Chloris, the earth with water that   20
I've drawn from fountains three; this altar new
That I have built from earth, with herbs, wind round
Three times, and with soft ribbands four times round;
Then incense masculine and chaste vervain[83]
Set you alight and in   25

Dirai: così s'accenda
Quel cor, ch'è per noi fatto un freddo gielo.
Torni il mio Tirsi al primo nostro amore.

In varie, e strane forme
Ben possono gli incanti   30
Cangiar gli huomini, e ponno
Fermar de' fiumi il corso
Trar dal bosco le fiere,
Gli angui dai fior, fuori del centro l'ombre,
E la Luna dal Cielo.   35
Torni il mio Tirsi al primo nostro amore.

Quel cor fatto di cera ò Clori prendi,
Ed affigivi dentro
Questi aghi, e queste spine;
E dì: sì punga il core   40
Di lui strale d'Amore.
Getta nel foco il crepitante alloro,
E misto con quel core il farro, e'l sale,
Dona à le sacre fiamme,
Acciòch'egli per me non men si strugga,   45

Che la cera nel foco; e mal suo grado
Mi segua, e'n me sospiri;
E più mi brami, che bramar non suole
Vago augellin dopo la pioggia il Sole.
Di tre veli diversi i nodi stringi,   50
E tre volte dirai:
Così stringer poss'io
Tutti i pensier di quello,
Che tutti i miei pensier chiude nel seno.
Torni il mio Tirsi al primo nostro amore.   55

Quì sopra questa foglia
Scrivo di Tirsi il nome;
Ma di Venere prima
Il possente carattere io vi segno.
Del suo bel corpo amato   60

A deep voice say, "Thus may
That heart catch fire that's cold as ice towards us.
Return, my Thyrsis, to our former love.

"In strange and varied ways
Can incantations make   30
Men change, indeed, and can
Make rivers cease to flow,
Draw wild beasts from the woods,
Draw snakes from flowers, from earth's center, shades,
And from the sky the moon.   35
Return, my Thyrsis, to our former love."

"This heart that's made of wax, O Chloris, take,
And then transfix it midst
These needles and these thorns;
And say: "So let the darts   40
Of Love pierce through his heart."
Throw in the fire the crackling laurel then,
And mixed with that heart throw spelt; and salt as well[84]
Give to the sacred flames,
So he may melt for me no less than does   45

This wax in fire; and, never mind his will,
Pursue me, sigh for me;
May he, unused to yearning, pine for me
As after rain sweet songbirds long for sun.
Tie knots together from three different veils,   50
And then three times repeat:
Like this I can knot up
That fellow's every thought,
For all my thoughts in his breast are enclosed.
Return, my Thyrsis, to our former love."   55

"And here upon this leaf
I write down Thyrsis's name;
But first this potent sign,
The symbol of Venus I outline for you.
Next trace the longed-for spoils   60

Le amate spoglie poi,
Che per mesta memoria m'avanzaro
De la sua fuga, io pongo
Confuse quì con la segnata fronda;
E perche meglio à voti miei risponda   65
Il magico sussurro
Questi capegli, ch'io
Lievemente tagliai
Da la sua bionda innannellata chioma
Mentr'egli nel mio sen dolce dormìa   70
Sacro devota à questa
Soglia vedova, e mesta;
Perch'ella à me'l richiami,
Ed amato pur m'ami.
Torni il mio Tirsi al primo nostro amore.   75

Hor sopra'l foco leggiermente io spargo
Questo vino spumante.
Strida come l'acceso
Carbon, quell'empio, e rìo,
Che di nostra sventura hor tanto gode.   80
Questo liquor da le premute olive
Tratto, nel seno io verso.
Del foco già vicino
A rimaner estinto;
Ed ecco ei torna più che mai cocente;   85
Così ritorni ardente
Del mio bel Sol la fiamma
In cui già visse dolcemente ardendo.
Torni il mio Tirsi al primo nostro amore.
Premi quell'herbe tal che fuor ne venga   90
Il velenoso humore, à cui di Ponto
Cede ogn'altro velen: così da Tirsi
Esca la crudeltà velen del core,
Che'n lui si trova, e me dolente attosca.
Torni il mio Tirsi al primo nostro amore.   95

Of his dear body fine;
Because the painful memory of his flight
Hung over me, I place
Remorse here alongside this figured leaf;
And just because the magic whisper may   65
Respond the better to
My prayers and offerings,
"These hairs which nimbly I
Have snipped from his blond, charming, curly mane,
While he was sweetly sleeping in my arms,   70
I solemnly devote to this
Sad widow all alone;
So that she'll call him back to me,
And he, beloved, will love me still.
Return, my Thyrsis, to our former love."   75

"Now gingerly I sprinkle on the fire
This foaming wine, and, like
This coal I burn, may that
One, wicked, vile, cry out
Who takes in our misfortune such great joy,   80
This liquor that I've drawn from olives pressed
I spill upon my breast."
The fire is very near
To being doused; when, lo,
More searing than before, it flares again;   85
"Thus may he come back burning,
The flame of my fair sun
In which I once lived sweetly, all aflame.
Return, my Thyrsis, to our former love.
"Those herbs, squeeze so their humors poisonous   90
Flow out of them, for they are Pontine and
Surpass all other banes; From Thyrsis's heart
Let thus flow forth the poison cruelty
That's found in him and woefully kills me.
Return, my Thyrsis, to our former love.   95

Questo incantato ferro intorno io volgo
Perche'l mio Tirsi à me pur volga il piede
Ardendo in me sicome avampo in lui.
Torni il mio Tirsi a primo nostro amore.

Discinta, e scalza intorno al sacro Altare   100
Tre volte io giro, e tre la chioma scuoto,
Tre volte io bacio questa ignuda terra;
E prego il Ciel, s'invida Ninfa, ò Dèa
Mi spoglia del mio ben, ch'ella in se stessa
Provi del mio gran duol l'estremo oltraggio.   105
Torni il mio Tirsi al primo nostro amore.

Prendi quelle, che al vento
Lucertole seccai,
E quelle in polve già serpi converse;
E con quel cener freddo   110
Confondi tutto, e mesci;
Poi con ambe le man prendile; e come
Gettaron l'ossa de la madre Antica
Deucalione, e Pirra
Gettale Clori tù nel vicin fiume;   115
E dì con alta voce.
Così ne porti l'onda
De la compagna mia gli egri martìri.
Torni il mio Tirsi al primo nostro amore.

Un Fonte è tal, che chi quell'acqua beve   120
D'ardentissimo amor l'anima accende,
Ne beva Tirsi, e'n me sospiri, ed arda.
Un Rege fù, la cui terrena spoglia
In augello cangiar gli eterni Dei,
E di sì varie, e vaghe penne è sparso,   125
Che sembra ancor haver d'intorno il manto,
E la corona hà pur di penne; il nido
Have di questo augel pietra sì rara,
Che chiunque l'ottiene amato è sempre
Da quella per cui porta il cor piagato;   130

"This iron enchanted thus I turn about;
So may my Thyrsis turn his foot toward me,
Burning in me as I'm ablaze in him.
Return, my Thyrsis to our former love.

"Half-nude and barefoot, thrice I circle round   100
The sacred altar; thrice I toss my hair,
And thrice I kiss this naked earth, and ask
The sky, if some invidious nymph
Or goddess rob me of my good,
That she may feel the awful outrage of my woe.   105
Return, my Thyrsis to our former love.

"Take those lizards that
I've dried out in the wind,
And mix them, yes, of course, with serpent dust;
And, with that, ashes cold.   110
Stir everything mixed well;
Then with both your hands take them, and, as
Deucalion and Pyrrha hurled the bones
Of their old mother; O,[85]
Throw them, Chloris, in the river near.   115
And with a loud voice say:
'Thus may the waves bear off
The sickly torments my companion feels.
Return, my Thyrsis, to our former love.'

"A spring there is whose waters, when one drinks,   120
Sets him aflame with a most ardent love;
Let Thyrsis drink it, sigh for me, and burn.
There was a king whose earthly body was
By the eternal gods changed to a bird,
Of such a species with fair feathers fletched   125
That still he seemed to wear his royal cloak,
And even seemed to wear a feathered crown;
Of such rare stone was made this bird's nest that
Whoever obtained it was forever loved
By her for whom he bore a wounded heart;   130

Deh porgi à me pietosa Luna questa
Mirabil pietra; accioche Tirsi mio
Non ricusi d'amarme, che l'adoro.
Deh porgi ò Luna à' nostri incanti aìta.

Tù pur in sogno à la famosa Elpina   135
Dotta à l'indovinar con l'onda pura,
E col foco, e col cribro
Di Circe, e di Medea
E l'herbe, e i sassi, e le parole, e i carmi
Insegnasti cortese;   140
Ed ella à noi poscia insegnolli: hor sieno
Valide homai queste fatiche nostre.
Deh porgi ò Luna à' nostri incanti aìta.

Tù, ch'adorata se' ne gli alti Monti
Deh non mi riguardar con torvo ciglio.   145
O de le stelle chiaro, e bel Pianeta,
O splendor de la notte,
O del Ciel maggior lume dopo quello
Del tuo biondo fratello
Il cor selvaggio, e crudo   150
Vinci del crudo Tirsi, e s'unquà amasti
Pietà del dolor mio l'alma ti punga.
Deh porgi ò Luna à' nostri incanti aìta.

Prestami il tuo favor, fà, che l'ingrato
Ritorni à farsi amante, e la sua parte   155
Habbia anch'egli del foco, ond'io tutt'ardo.
Sgombra da lui la natural fierezza,
Fà, che benigno le pietose orecchie
Porga a' miei giusti preghi,
E pietà non mi neghi.   160
Deh porgi ò Luna à' nostri incanti aìta.

Hor se'l tuo volto eternamente scopra
Gli argentati suoi raggi, e de le nubi
Rompano la caligine profonda,
Onde con bianche, e pure corna il Cielo   165

Ah please bestow on me, O piteous moon,
This marvelous stone, so Thyrsis, whom I so
Adore, can make no choice except for loving me.
Ah, on our magic, Moon, bestow your aid!

"O Moon, you courteously in dreams have taught 135
The learned Elpina (who's so renowned)
Soothsaying with pure waves,
And with the fire as well,
With Circe's sieve and with Medea's herbs,
With rocks and words and songs!— 140
And she has taught us these things afterwards.
Now, these our labors, let them work their spell.
Ah, on our magic, Moon, bestow your aid!

"You, Moon, who in high mountains are adored,
Ah do not look on me with threatening brow. 145
O bright among the stars, O planet fair,
O splendor of the night,
O major light of Heaven after that
Of your blond brother bright,
Subdue the savage heart 150
Of Thyrsis cruel, and, if ever you ever loved,
Let pity for my sorrow pierce your soul.
Ah, on our magic, Moon, bestow your aid!

"Lend me your favor, make that ingrate come
Again to make a lover of himself, and let 155
Him also have his share of flame with which
I'm all consumed. His native fierceness sweep
Away. Let him be kind and pitying,
Lend ear to my just prayers
And not deny me ruth. 160
Ah, on our magic, Moon, bestow your aid!

"Now if your face eternally reveals
Your silvery beams, rays that are breaking through
The clouds' dense vapors, after which you sail
Rotating every hour through the sky 165

Tu vada ogn'hor rotando;
Nè mai Pastor de' baci tuoi se n'vada
Per gli alti monti altero,
Concedi à me dolente,
E sconsolata amante   170
Quel, che pregando io chiedo.
Deh porgi ò Luna à' nostri incanti aìta.

Senti ò mia Clori, senti,
Ch'abbaia il fido cane.
Certo questo latrar è buon'augurio,   175
O pur m'insegna amor crederlo tale;
Amor, che di menzogne il mio cor pasce.
Tirsi non veggio (ohime) non veggio il Sole,
Che le tenebre mie sgombrar solèa.
M'accorgo ben, che son gli incanti vani,   180
E più vana è colei, che dà lor fede.
Falso prodigio di verace doglia
E'l bugiardo latrar, c'hor mi dimostra,
Che'l vero amor non con incanti, od herbe,
Ma con beltà, ma con vertù s'acquista.   185

With your horns, white and pure;
Or if ever a shepherd, for your kisses, trekked
Through mountains proud and high,
To me a lover sad,
Disconsolate, O grant   170
What I in prayer request.
Ah, on our magic, Moon, bestow your aid!"

"Listen, O my Chloris, hear
The baying of the faithful dog."
"An omen good this howling surely is—   175
At least, Love teaches me to think it so—
That Love who nourishes my heart with lies.
Not seeing Thyrsis, I don't see the Sun
(Oh me!) that used to clear my shadows off.
I'm well aware that magic spells are vain,   180
And vainer still is she who credits them.
A false phantasm of a sorrow true
Is that misleading howl you note for me,
For true love can't be had with spells or herbs,
With beauty and with virtue it is gained."   185

Notes

1. *Thyrsis*: Idealized Greek shepherd; see, Theocritus, *Idyll* I; Virgil, *Bucolics* 7.
2. *Chiabrera*: (1552-1638), a great lyric poet of the age who reacted against the conventionalities of Petrarchism.
3. In the Italian Andreini names the winds: Boreus (the north wind), Eurus (the southeast wind), and Notus (Auster, the south wind).
4. Neptune was god of the earthquake as well as of the sea.
5. *realms to Realms*: Ital. Regni à regni: Rulers leave their realms to other rulers and to the disposition of eternity.
6. *Marsyas*, a satyr, found the flute that the goddess Athena had invented and discarded. He became a virtuoso and challenged Apollo to a contest. Marsyas lost, and Apollo flayed him alive. Andreini's graceful compliment suggests that unlike Marsyas, Chiabrera would defeat Apollo in a similar contest.
7. *Clio*: The muse of history.
8. *Amadigi*: Amadis of Gaul—a knight of the court of Charlemagne whose name became the title and who was subject of several poems and operas.
9. *Permessus' peak*: Mt. Helicon, which overlooks Permessus, a river valley sacred to the Muses.
10. *Delius*: An alternate name for Phoebus Apollo, the sun god. A major center of his worship was on the island of Delos.
11. *Amphion*: One of the twin rulers of Thebes, Amphion and his brother Zethus were the sons of Zeus and Antiope. Amphion was such an accomplished harper that his music helped build the walls of Thebes by drawing the stones into their places. Andreini compares the force of Chiabrera's music to the effect of Amphion's. Liguria is the area along the western coast of Italy that centers on Genoa.
12. *Red Sea*, etc.: The rivers and sea of the first quatrain are those of the Near East and Asia. Those of lines 9-11 are European rivers, except for the Hermus, which is in Turkey. The waters named in line 12 are all in Italy.
13. *cloister low*: this world.
14. *Cinthio*: Cardinal San Giorgio Cinthio Aldobrandini, leader of the Italian Counter Reformation and the person to whom Andreini dedicated her lyrics.

15. *water . . . flame*: alludes to the humors—the liquid versions of the four elements of Greek physics: earth, air, fire, and water, one or the other of which was thought to predominate in each human body and to be the principal determinant of personality. Circulating in the human body these liquids were, respectively, black bile, yellow bile, blood, and phlegm. The "falling humor" (line 13) alludes to tears.

16. *these plants*: Apparently this Sestina was composed to accompany a gift of plants.

17. *Castor and Pollux*: Legendary figures sometimes thought to have been born from the union of Zeus in the form of a swan and Leda. Castor and Pollux were worshiped as gods in Roman times; they were thought to have been stellified as the stars in the constellation Gemini. These stars point toward the north star and could be used for navigation. Those in Orion, since they appeared to move across the horizon, could not.

18. Francesco Petrarca, *Petrarch's Songbook: Rerum vulgarium fragmenta* [hereafter *Rerum*], trans. James Wyatt Cook (Binghamton, NY: Medieval Renaissance Texts and Studies, Vol. 151, State University of New York at Binghamton, 1996) 14:12 (references are to poem and line number).

19. *Rerum*, 326:1.

20. *Rerum*: 170:7.

21. *Rerum*: 13:4.

22. *Rerum*: 278:4

23. *Rerum*: 156:3.

24. *Rerum*: 17:1.

25. *Rerum*: 67:4.

26. *Rerum*: 226:5.

27. *Rerum*: 183:11.

28. *Rerum*: 1:6.

29. *Rerum*: 360:34.

30. *Rerum*: 337:11.

31. *Rerum*: 283:8.

32. *Rerum*: 35:2.

33. *Rerum*: 280:6

34. *Rerum*: 266:3.

35. *Rerum*: 93:14.

36. *Rerum*: 109:4.

37. *Rerum*: 125:24.

38. *Rerum*: 292:1.
39. *Rerum*: 274:1.
40. *Rerum*: 108:4.
41. *Rerum*: 66:25.
42. *Rerum*: 209:5.
43. *Rerum*: 325:108.
44. *Rerum*: 321:5.
45. *Rerum*: 196:14.
46. *Rerum*: 251:10.
47. *Rerum*: 174:9.
48. *Rerum*: 161:11.
49. *Iris*: Goddess of the rainbow in Greek mythology.
50. This is a wonderful image in the Italian. "Vibrare" in this context catches both the warlike shaking or brandishing of weapons and the shimmering of heat waves.
51. Lesbin, a shepherd, and Nisida, a nymph.
52. *Hybla*: A town in Sicily famed for its honey.
53. *Aurora*: Goddess of the dawn who, in the amorous vernacular tradition, is responsible for the unwilling separation of lovers.
54. *kerchiefs*, Ital., *bende*: These were headdresses worn in various colors by married women, but exclusively in white by widows.
55. *Rinuccini*: (1562-1621) A poet and librettist whose *Eurydice* was, in the year 1600, twice set to music by composers Jacopo Peri (1561-1633) and Giulio Caccini (ca. 1545-1618) and performed in Florence. Andreini's poem recounts the opera's plot.
56. *Clio*: The muse of history.
57. *Lucchesini*: A singer and dear friend of Andreini.
58. *Thessaly, Sorgue*: Here the name of the Greek region Thessaly alludes to the myth of Apollo and Daphne. Apollo fell in love with the Thessalian nymph Daphne and pursued her. She prayed for help and Zeus turned her into a laurel tree. The laurel leaf is an emblem of victory and immortality. In his *Rerum vulgarium fragmenta*, the Italian poet Francesco Petrarch (1304-1374) used the same myth as an emblem of his love for Laura and his pursuit of fame and immortality. For a part of his life, Petrarch lived in Vaucluse near Avignon, a valley where the Sorgue river has its source. This is one of many poems in which Andreini draws inspiration from the work, *topoi*, and images of Petrarch. The point here is that in her beauty and talents, Laura Guidiccioni Lucchesini surpassed both Apollo's Daphne and Petrarch's Laura.

59. *Rerum*: 311:11.
60. *Rerum*: 245:1.
61. *Rerum*: 323:30.
62. *Rerum*: 325:47.
63. *Rerum*: 183:10.
64. *Rerum*: 292:6.
65. *Rerum*: 17:1.
66. *Rerum*: 323:72.
67. *Rerum*: 270:107.
68. *Rerum*: 323:72.
69. *Rerum*: 278:13.
70. *Rerum*: 239:25.
71. *Rerum*: 278:4.
72. *Rerum*: 332:42.
73. *Paris*: A Trojan prince and shepherd who was loved by the nymph Oenone. Foolishly, Paris agreed to judge a beauty contest in which the contestants were Aphrodite, goddess of love; Athena, goddess of wisdom; and Hera, goddess of power. Each goddess tried to bribe him. Paris accepted Aphrodite's bribe, the love of the world's most beautiful woman—a prize he later claimed by running away with Helen of Troy, wife of King Menelaus of Sparta.
74. *Clio*: See n. 56.
75. *Prometheus*: The Titan who in Greek myth shapes human beings out of clay and is punished by the gods for bringing fire to people.
76. *old flame*: See Virgil, Dido's remark in *Aeneid* 4:23, and Dante *Purgatorio* xxx: 48.
77. *Tasso*: Torquato Tasso (1544-1595) was one of the greatest epic poets of his age.
78. *swan*: A conventional symbol for a poet.
79. *Clio*: See n. 56.
80. With this sonnet a series of spiritual poems begins.
81. The story of God's mercy toward Nineveh is found in the book of Jonah.
82. *nighttime sun*: moonlight.
83. *Vervain*: A herb, *verbena officinalis*, used here in a love charm.
84. *spelt*: *Triticum spelta*, a grain.
85. *Deucalion-mother*: In the Greek version of the flood story, Deucalion, son of Prometheus, and Deucalion's wife, Pyrrha, threw stones (the bones of their mother, earth) over their shoulders. Those thrown by

Deucalion turned into men and those by Pyrrha to women, thus repopu-
lating the earth.

Chapter 3
Selections from
Rime d'Isabella Andreini
comica gelosa, & academica intenta
detta l'Accesa. Parte seconda
(1605)

Sonnetto Primo
All'illustrissimo & Reverendissimo Signor Cardinale
Cinthio Aldobrandini

Di sdegnoso rossor Febo t'accendi
(Ben lo conosco) e quando sorgi, e quando
I veloci destrier nel Mar tuffando
A Theti in sen precipitoso scendi;   4

Perche mentre lo sguardo acuto intendi
À questo Sol, che'l Mondo hor va beando
Co' purissimi rai, d'ira avampando,
La tua luce homai vinta a sdegno prendi.   8

La tua luce qui vela, ò de le grotte
Cimerie l'ombra, ó fosca nube, ó s'ella
Fiammeggia; non risplende ad ogni gente.   11

Dicanlo quei, che da sì lunga notte
Oppressi stan; ma in questa parte, e in quella
CINTHIO scopre ad ogni hor suo raggio ardente.   14

Sonnet 1
To the most illustrious and most reverend Lord Cardinal
Cinthio Aldobrandini

Flushed red with ire, O Phoebus, you're ablaze
(I know it well) both when you rise, and when,
Your speedy chargers plunging in the sea,
To Thetis's bosom swiftly you sink down.[1]   4

For while you turn your piercing gaze upon
This sun that now brings blessing to the world
With purest rays, aflame with wrath,
You're filled with ire that your light's vanquished now.   8

"Either the shadow of Avernan caves,
Or a dark cloud here veils your light, or if
It flames; it shines not on all folk."   11

Thus say those who by such a long night are
Oppressed; but every hour in these parts
And those, CINTHIO reveals his ardent ray.[2]   14

Madrigale III

Qual dispietato artiglio il cor mi svelle?
Qual incendio mi sface,
Nel lasciar l'alta, e risplendente face   3
Di queste amiche Stelle?
Lasso pur giungo al fin del viver mio,
Tanto può del partir l'amaro addio.   6

Madrigale IV

Qualhor miro l'argento
Di lei, ch'è de la notte unico Sole,
Di lei, ch'è de le Stelle almo ornamento
Par, che desio d'amor nel sen mi vole,
Par, ch'una dolce invidia haggia nel petto,   5
Fortunato Pastor del tuo contento.
Anch'io baci vorrei
Da quella Dea, che regge i pensier miei;
Ma desto, ond'anco à lei baci rendessi
Con gli strali d'amor ne' baci impressi.   10

Madrigale V

Morrò crudel, morrò, ma nel morire
Questo disperatissimo conforto
Havrò; che ben, che à torto
M'uccidan fiero i tuoi disdegni, e l'ire,
Ne i detti, e ne i sembianti   5
Non si vedrà l'interno mio dolore,
Nè, ch'i' chieda pietà sia, che ti vanti.
Generoso mio core,
Morte dolce, e gradita,
Che sdegni haver del mio nemico aita.   10

Madrigal 3

What ruthless claw is tearing out my heart?
What firestorm ruins me
In leaving the lofty and resplendent sight   3
Of all these friendly stars?
Alas, I'll surely come to my life's end,
So bitter can this farewell be at parting.   6

Madrigal 4

Whenever upon her silver face
I gaze, on hers who is the only Sun
Of night, who is the Stars' life-giving jewel.[3]
It seems I feel love's longing in my breast;
It seems I have sweet envy in my heart,   5
O lucky shepherd, of your happiness.[4]
Kisses from that goddess who
Commands my every thought I too would wish;
But quickly, while you still were kissing her,
You tipped your kisses with the darts of Love.   10

Madrigal 5

I shall die, O cruel one, I shall die,
But, dying, this most hopeless comfort shall
I have; for wrongfully,
Fierce one, your wrath and scorn are killing me,
And in my words and looks   5
My inner sorrow will not be perceived,
Nor will your boasting when I beg for ruth.
O my generous heart,
Death is welcome, sweet,
For you disdain help from my enemy.   10

Sonetto XXXII
Del Sig. Gio. Battista Marini
Vedendo recitare una Tragedia all'Autrice I. A.

Spettator del mio mal, son hoggi intento
Doppio Theatro à vagheggiar rivolto,
Un me ne scopre il tragico ornamento,
Un me ne mostra in breve spatio un volto.   4

Nel un stupido veggio, e lieto ascolto
Vaghe pitture, e musico concento;
Ne l'altro il bel del Paradiso accolto,
E'l parlar de le Gratie ammiro, e sento   8

In quel, di faci luminose splende.
Ricca pompa notturna: in questo Amore,
Vincitrici del Sol due luci accende.   11

Là, d'huom, che pur non senza colpa more,
L'acerbo fin; Quì, la mia mente attende
La morte (ohime) de l'inocente core.   14

Sonnet 32
By Mr. Gio. Battista Marino[5]
On seeing performed a tragedy by its author, I. A.

An observer of my ill today, I turned
To watch a double theater unfold;
The one shows me its tragic ornaments—
One its face to me will shortly bare.   4

In one, amazed, I watch exquisite scenes
And, joyful, hear harmonious music played;
Edenic beauty in the other I
See gleaned, and hear the Graces spoken of,   8

And hear, in that, of splendid glowing deeds—
Of rich nocturnal pomp—in this of Love,
See two enkindled lights outshine the sun.   11

There, hear of man, who does not guiltless die—
The bitter end; here, my mind waits the death
(Ah, woe is me) of my heart, innocent.   14

Sonetto XXXIII
Risposta al Sig. Gio. Battista Marini

Care gemme d'Apollo onde il mio giorno
Ogn'hora tragge homai ricca, e serena.
Rime soavi, ogni mio spirto affrena
Vostro canoro stil di cui m'adorno.   4

Per voi pompa, e splendor veggiom' intorno,
E cangiarsi in diletto ogni mia pena
Mentre sudando in faticosa Scena
Langue il Tempo ferito, e pien di scorno,   8

Saettato da voi, cui sono Ancelle
Riverenti le Muse; ei nel profondo
Lethe bestemmi opre sì rare, e belle.   11

Tù alzi ò MARIN co'l suon giocondo
Altri da terra à le dorate Stelle,
Vincendo me, già vincitor del Mondo.   14

Sonnet 33
Reply to Mr. Gio. Battista Marino

Gems precious of Apollo whence my day
At every hour henceforth grows rich and bright,
Soft rhymes, the style melodious with which you
Adorn me wholly takes my breath away.[6]   4

Through you I see around me splendor, pomp,
And into delight my every pain is turned;
While sweating on the weary, spiteful stage,
Time suffers wounded, filled with scorn, pierced through   8

By you, whose reverent handmaids the Muses are.
In Lethe's depths let Time work so: let him
Curse all such works so lovely and so rare.[7]   11

You raise, Marini, with your joyous sound,
People to the golden stars from earth,
Conquering me, the conqueror of the world.[8]   14

Sonetto XXXVI
Alla Christianissima Regina di Francia
Maria de' Medici

A le rose, che in Cielo apre l'Aurora,
Et à i gigli la porpora, e'l candore
Del bel volto agguagliar deggio, ond'Amore
Se stesso, non ch'altri dolce inamora?   4

Nò; che sol pari à se fuga, e scolora
L'alba, non che sue pompe, e divo ardore
Spira d'HENRICO al generoso core
La real Donna, e i suoi trionfi honora: 8

E voi di strali armati, occhi divini,
Le spoglie havete pur tante, e sì rare
Di lui, che vince il Dio de l'armi in guerra.   11

Dritto è ben ch'ogni età lieta v'inchini
Lucidissimi rai, quand'hoggi appare
Per voi non men del Ciel vaga la Terra.   14

Madrigale IX

In questo c'hor t'invio
Nobil cristallo, e schietto
Ò bella, O saggia mia prendi l'humore
Di chiaro, e fresco Rio.
Indi trarrai dal petto,
E la sete, e l'ardore;   6
Se poi di me pietosa
La mia sete amorosa, e'l foco ardente
Vuoi far men grave al core
A la mia bocca, O mio bel Sol lucente,
Il dolce labbro tuo porgi sovente.   11

Sonnet 36
To the most Christian Queen of France
Maria de' Medici[9]

To crimson roses Aurora opens in heaven,
To lilies white must I compare your face
So fair that it enamors Love himself,
Let alone others who fall in love with it?   4

Ah no, for dawn flees the comparison—
Not just her splendors fade; the godlike honor of
His royal lady Henry's generous heart
Inspires, and to his triumphs honor brings.   8

You eyes divine, too, you with arrows armed,
Have even greater spoils for him, so rare
He even subdues the god of arms in war.   11

It's surely right that you your brightest rays
On every age should bend, when earth it seems
By you is graced no less than Heaven is graced.   14

Madrigal 9

In this I send you now,
A noble crystal pure,
O my wise, lovely one, sip water from
A cool, clear rivulet.
Thus from your breast you'll draw
Both thirst and heat as well;   6
If then you pity me,
And wish to make less grave my amorous thirst
And my heart's ardent fire,
On my mouth, O my lovely, shining Sun,
Press frequently that honeyed lip of yours.   11

Madrigale X

In saldissimo gielo
Le mie lagrime triste si cangiarò,
Indi girando il Cielo
Cristallo diventato
Di cui formossi questo Vaso poi,
Hor tù ch'altro non vuoi   6
Bella Tigre, che'l pianto de gli amanti
Quì li raccogli, e godi
Che in non più intesi modi
Di tanti (ahi cruda) c'hai piagati e tanti
Il pianto havrai ne' congelati pianti.   11

Madrigale XI

Avara, liberal, cruda, e pietosa
Vaga NISIDA mia ti scopro à un tempo.
A la fame amorosa
Involi del bel seno i dolci pomi;
E ne l'istesso tempo,   5
Perche'l digiun del corpo io vinca, e domi
De' tuoi ricchi giardini altri men' porgi.
Ma come non t'accorgi,
Che mentre cibi il corpo (ahi lasso) il core
Per soverchio digiun languisce, e more?   10

Madrigal 10

Into ice most solid were
These woeful tears of mine transformed and then
Went wheeling in the sky,
Turned into crystal next
From which this lovely vase was molded then.
Now you who nothing wish,   6
Except, my lovely tiger, lovers' tears,
Collect them here; rejoice
That in unheard of ways
You'll keep in frozen tears, ah cruel one,
The sobs of the many, many, you've wounded so.   11

Madrigal 11

Cruel, greedy, generous, and merciful,
Fair NISIDA I find that all at once
From my amorous hunger
The sweet apples of your lovely breast you hide;
In that same moment too,   5
So I might quell and tame my body's fast,
You offered other fruit from your rich groves.
But how can you not see
That while you feed my body (woe!) my heart
Through unremitting fasting starves to death.   10

Sonetto XLIV

Al Principe di Condè
Henrico di Borbon
Gran Principe di Francia

Principe del sangue

O Di Pianta Real vago, e sublime
Ramo, da cui spuntar si veggon fuori,
E di speme, e di gioia, e frondi, e fiori;
Qual'altro fia ch'al par di te si stime?   4

Veggio Apollo per te Lasciar le cime
Del bicorne Parnaso; odo gli honori
Tuoi nel suo canto, e sì bearne i cori,
Che'l Tempo ogn'hor sia che se'n rodi, e lime.   8

Pargoletto gentil come di gloria
Frutti non produrrai, se'l Tronco altero
Nel terren di virtù tien la radice?   11

Così t'arrida il Ciel come d'Historia
Degno sarai, come per te felice
Tornerà il Mondo al bel viver primiero.   14

Sonnet 44

To the Prince of Condè
Henry of Bourbon
The Great Prince of France

Prince of the blood

O branch sublime of the fair royal tree
At whose appearance one sees open forth
The flower and the leaf of hope and joy,
Who can esteem himself to be your peer?   4

For you I see Apollo leave the top
Of twin-peaked Parnassus; in his song
I hear your honors; choirs so bless them that
For them, Time's wrath will gnaw him, wear him down.   8

O noble child, how can you not produce
The fruits of glory, if the lofty trunk
In virtue's ground is firmly rooted fast?   11

Just as you're worthy of history, let Heaven smile
On you since for you the happy world will turn
To the fine life of the golden age once more.[10]   14

Sonetto XLVIII
A Monsieur le Grand

Fuor de l'onde trahea sereno il giorno
Febo; quando benigno in te l'aspetto
Volse ogni Stella; onde tu solo oggetto
Di lor te'n vai di mille gratie adorno.   4

Vaghe d'honor ti fan corona intorno
Dotte schiere, sua pompa, e suo diletto
SENNA t'appella; e d'amoroso affetto
Arde per te ne l'humido soggiorno.   8

Chi più tra noi risplende, e chi felice
In terra è più? chi vide in human velo
Folgorar di virtù più ardenti rai?   11

Ben è ver, che di te cantar non lice;
Che'l tuo merto gentil vince d'assai
O grato à i Regi, e viè più grato al Cielo.   14

Sonnet 48
To Mr. le Grand

The bright day, Phoebus, rises from the waves
When every star its favorable aspect's turned
On you; whence you go on your way, the stars'
Sole object, with a thousand graces decked.   4

Seeking honor, the learned throng press in
Around you, and the Seine calls you its pride
And its delight, and in its watery course
It burns for you with feelings amorous.   8

Among us who shines brighter? Who on earth
Is happier? Who sees more ardent rays
Of virtue through a human veil blaze forth?   11

It's surely true that its not right to sing
Of you, because your noble merit more will win,
You, prized by kings, and there in Heaven prized more.   14

Alla medesima

Sopra l'Historia di Madamoisella di Chiaramonte
Sonetto LV

Tu con leggiadra insolita vaghezza
Donna, anzi di virtù Mostro gentile
Narri, che per amor Donna virile
D'acuto, e rio velen la forza sprezza.   4

Hor noi mentre ammiriam l'egregia altezza
(Chi'l crederà) del tuo canoro stile
Prende l'alma (ogn'altra esca havend'à vile)
Velen cui sparge Amor d'alta dolcezza.   8

Tua CHIARAMONTE che per te resplende
Viè più chiara ch'l Sol, vivendo trova
Rimedio al fin, ch'al tosco la sottragge.   11

Ma quel tosco d'amor, che in voi rinova,
De la filtra il poter, rimedio attende
Quand'uscirem de le mondane spiagge.   14

To the same
(Caterina di Bourbon)
On the *History* of Mademoiselle di Clairemont
Sonnet 55

O Lady, with unusually charming grace,
Or rather with virtue, noble prodigy,
You say that a manly woman scorns for love
The wicked power of poison, bitter, sharp.   4

Now while we admire the noble loftiness
(Who'd credit it!) of your sweet style, one takes
(Though any other bait's thought vile) for its
High sweetness the vital poison Love spreads round.   8

Your CLAIREMONT, who for you is shining bright,
Far brighter than the sun, alive will find
For the bane that sickens her an antidote   11

At last. Love's poison though, which she renews
In you by her potion's power, for remedy
Will wait until we leave these worldly shores.   14

Sonetto LXIX
Sopra *La Corrente*, Ballo nel quale i Cavalieri rubano le Dame

È Danza, ò pugna questa? ecco s'io miro
Mover Dive, & Heroi con arte il vago
Leggiadro piè, di lieti balli appago
Il cor, ne chiede altr'esca il mio desiro.   4

Se predar veggio in questo breve giro
La bella amica al valoroso vago.
Scorgo del Frigio involator l'imago,
O di quei ch'à Sabini il bel rapiro.   8

Amore, e Marte han quì lor misto impero
L'un'arde, e l'altro invola, ed ambi il crine
Cingon fastose, ed honorate palme.   11

O fortunate, ò nobili rapine,
Com'hoggi fate il gran trionfo altero
Vincendo Marte i corpi, ed Amor l'alme.   14

Madrigale XVII

Colma di fasto io me ne gia cantando,
Lungo un fiorito colle;
E quasi (o mia sciocchezza)
Godea di questa mia frale bellezza.
Quando frà l'herba molle   5
Vidi languir'un fiore
Privo del suo vital soave humore,
E conobbi, che tale
Era beltà mortale.   9

Sonnet 69
About *La Corrente*, a ballet in which the knights steal the women

Is this a battle or a dance? Lo, if I watch
The goddesses and heroes move with skill
Their graceful, nimble feet, I please my heart
With joyous dance, and no bait else asks my   4

Desire. If in this brief whirl I observe
The valorous lover carry his sweetheart off,
Scenes of the Phrygian rapists I behold,
Or those who stole the Sabine men's delight.   8

Love and Mars have joined their empires here,
One burns, the other steals, and both bind round
Their locks the splendid and the venerated palms.   11

O you abductions noble, fortunate,
How great a triumph proud you've made today,
Mars vanquishes your bodies, Love your souls.   14

Madrigal 17

Glutted with splendor and singing, indeed,
I went along a flowery hill
And I then almost (O,
My folly!) in this my beauty frail rejoiced.
When I saw drooping in   5
The dewy grass a flower
Denied its vivifying liquid sweet,
And mortal loveliness,
I knew, was of that sort.   9

Madrigale XVIII

"Dimmi, lasso mio core,
Quand'havrà fine il mio sí lungo errore?"
"Incauta, come vuoi
Ch'habbiano fine, i miei martiri, e i tuoi,
Se di me ti privasti,   5
Et á chi non mi volse, m'inviasti?
Ei non mi vuol; tu mi ricusi: ond'io
Odio lo stato mio."
"Dunque non havrà fin sì dura sorte?"
"Non havrà fin giamai, se non per morte."   10

Sonetto LXXI
Al Sepolcro del Sannazaro in Napoli

Hor che'l dotto Sincero estinto giace,
Sebeto è privo de' suoi prischi honori,
D'altra Zampogna al suon gli agresti amori
Ad ogni agreste dio cantar dispiace.   4

Mesta ne gli altri Echo languisce, e tace;
Piangon le Valli, i Boschi, i Prati, i Fiori
Sdegna le Ninfe Amor; fugge i Pastori;
Spezza gli strali suoi, spezza la face.   8

Lucifero già fosti, Hespero hor sei,
Ch'ancor dopo l'Ocaso al mondo splendi
Saggio Pastor, ch'in breve marmo hor posi.   11

Alma gentil gli ardenti sospir miei
(Dicea FILLI dolente) in grado prendi
(Co' begli occhi di pianto rugiadosi.)   14

Madrigal 18

"Tell me, my weary heart,
When will my long, long error have an end?"
"Why think you, heedless one,
That both your pangs and mine should have an end
Since you got rid of me,   5
And, to where I wasn't wanted, made me go.
Me he wants not; you send me off; whence I
Hate my condition."
"Then such hard fate will never have an end?"
"It will not have an end except by death."   10

Sonnet 71
At the tomb of Sannazaro in Naples

Now that the learned Sincero lies deceased,[11]
Of its ancient honors Sebeto is stripped—[12]
The sound of his pastoral love songs played upon
Another pipe annoys each rustic god.   4

Among the others Echo faints, grows still;
The valleys weep, the woods, the meads and flowers,
Love shuns the nymphs, and Love the shepherds flees;
He breaks his arrows and puts out his torch.   8

Once Lucifer, indeed, you're Hesperus now,[13]
For, after setting, still you light the world,
Wise shepherd, though in marble now you rest.   11

O noble spirit, these ardent sighs of mine,
Take with good will (As woeful Phyllis said
"With lovely eyes, from weeping all bedewed.")   14

Sonetto LXXVIII
Del Sig. Angelo Ingegneri

In ischietto vestir vera bellezza,
Meglio riluce; e in verde prato herboso
Talhor viè più, che in bel giardino ombroso
Di Natura il valor s'ama, e s'aprezza,   4

Così, ben ch'habbia il favellar vaghezza
Quand egli, è di color ricco, e pomposo;
Più chiaro splende un'artificio ascoso,
Se pura il copre, e semplice dolcezza.   8

Donna, c'hor tutta bella, hor tutta ornata
Hor l'uno, e l'altro, i più contrari affetti
Con istupor altrui sempre imitate: 11

Di par ne gite ogn'hor chiara, e lodata:
Più forte al hor, che i bei soavi detti
Con minor arte, ò men palese usate.   14

Sonnet 78
By Mr. Angelo Ingegneri

When clothed in simple garb, true beauty shines
More bright; in grassy meadows, too, sometimes
There's more than in a shady garden fair.
One loves and prizes Nature's quality.   4

Just so, though, when a fine tale one would tell
And have it rich with color, splendor too,
More brightly shines a hidden artifice
When sweetness, pure and simple covers it.   8

O lady, now all lovely, florid now,
First this, then that, you always act for us
Feelings most opposite, dumbfound us all.   11

To see your work each hour grow bright, be praised—
More strongly now—let your fine, gentle words
Be used with less art, or less evident.   14

Risposta

Sonetto LXXIX

Un bel sembiante in habito negletto
Sua gratia perde; à i risguardanti è grato
Viè più colto giardin, che verde prato.
L'abborre Sol chi sprezza almo diletto.   4

Così più degno è pellegrin concetto,
Quand'altri di bei detti il rende ornato.
Ciò non tocca al mio dir, cui fù negato
Quel, che in te sol risplende, Angel perfetto.   8

Arte non hò, per ricoprir con l'arte
Mio stil, che in tutto di dolcezza priva
Loda non merta di celeste canto.   11

Deh saggio tù (se di lodarmi à schivo
Non hai) del vero dir pria dammi parte,
E confuso non sia co'l biasmo il vanto.   14

Response
(to Angelo Ingengneri)
Sonnet 79

A lovely figure in disheveled dress
Will lose its grace; and viewers will be pleased
With well-kept gardens more than with green meads.
One hates the sun who scorns sublime delight.   4

Just so, more worthy's an original idea
When varied, fine words make it elegant.
That, though, does not describe my censured verse—
That, perfect Angel, only shines in you.   8

I have no art to cover up my style
With an art that of all sweetness has been stripped,
An unbefitting praise for heavenly song.   11

Ah, wise you (if to praise me you aren't loath!)
To tell the truth, first give me what I'm due.
The praise won't be mistaken for the blame.   14

Sonetto LXXXIX
Del Sig. Ottavio Rinuccini, Invitando l'Autrice á cantar de la Sig. Cornelia Doni Gorini

Se in nobil Donna angelici sembianti,
S'honesto sguardo alteramente humile,
Se celesti pensieri, in cor gentile
Son degni pregi, onde ne scriva, e canti;   4

Udiran di CORNELIA il nome, e i vanti
Battro non pur, ma la remota Thile;
Ma sù l'ali n'andran de l'aureo stile
Oltra le nubi, oltra le Sfere erranti.   8

Se non fosser mie voglie à pianger volte,
Sol del nome di lei, per chiaro farmi,
Foran le carte mie vergate, e colte.   11

Tempra la Cetra tù; già d'udir parmi
Due rare meraviglie in un raccolte
Sue belle glorie, e tuoi leggiadri carmi.   14

Sonnet 89
From Mr. Ottavio Rinuccini, inviting the author to sing for Mrs. Cornelia Doni Gorini

If in a noble lady angelic ways,
And if a proudly humble glance, if thoughts
Celestial in a gentle heart deserve
One's praises, whence one writes and sings;   4

Not just Bactrus and Thule far away[14]
Will hear Cornelia's name and praises too;
But on the wings of aureate style they'll fly
Beyond the clouds, beyond the wandering spheres.   8

If my desires were not on weeping bent,
To make me cheerful, only with her name
Would I line my pages, gather them.   11

Tune up your lyre; already I seem to hear
Two marvels rare collected into one:
Her glories lovely and your enchanting songs.   14

Sonettto XC
Risposta

Sgombra dal ciglio homai gli amari pianti
O tu che'n dolce suon richiami Aprile
Tosco Anfion; Tu solo à te simile
Canta il bel volto, e gli atti, honesti, e santi.   4

Non hanno d'Ibla i fior tante Api, quanti
CORNELIA hà pregi, onde mia penna è vile;
Nè può qual'io vorrei tesser monile
Degno di girne à quei duo Soli avanti: 8

Non pensi una lodar: ma molte, e molte
Chi loda lei, che di virtute l'armi
Stringendo, have à l'età le forze tolte.   11

Al grave incarco hora convien sottrarmi:
Ma spero un dì, se sia che'l Ciel m'ascolte
Di sue glorie scrivendo eterna farmi.   14

Sonnet 90
Reply
(to Rinuccini)

Sweep from your eyelash now those bitter tears,
O you that with sweet strains call April back
To me, Tuscan Amphion; You, O peerless one,
Sing that fair face and chaste and lovely deeds.   4

Hybla's blooms have fewer bees than has
CORNELIA praises—for her my pen's too mean;
The necklace that I'd wish to weave for her
Can't worthily appear to those two suns.   8

Who praises her thinks not of just one praise,
But many, many, for, seizing virtue's arms,
She's taken all this epoch's powers herself.   11

I must refuse that heavy burden now,
But hope, if heaven hears me, one day I'll
Become immortal writing of her glories.   14

Sonnet XCIV
Del Sig. Cosimo Ruggieri, Abbate di S. Maghe in finibus terræ

S'a la vostra armonia bella Sirena,
A lo splendor, che folgorando luce
Ovvunque Apollo il dì colmo di luce
(Benche diverso) à tutti egual ne mena,   4

Cede l'alma inquieta, e mentre à pena
Se stessa à se dal vecchio foco adduce,
Non é colpa d'Amor, ne d'egli è Duce
Di sì ricco pensier, che in voi s'affrena.   8

Ma'l vostro almo splendor, ch'à poco, à poco
Da' sensi spezza il tenebroso velo,
E davvi (nova Musa) il primo loco;   11

Ch'à voi convien come'l rigore al gielo,
L'humido á l'onda, e come il caldo al foco,
La luce al Sole, e la vaghezza al Cielo.   14

Sonnet 94
From Mr. Cosimo Ruggieri, Abbot of St. Maggs at Land's End

If to your harmony, O Siren fair,
To the splendor that is flashing light
Wherever Apollo fills the day with light,
(Though different) brings it equally to all,   4

The restless soul submits, and while it can
But barely lead itself from the old fire,
It's not the fault of Love, nor is he guide
Of such lush thought, that in you is restrained.   8

But your life-giving splendor, bit by bit
From the senses rends the shadowy veil
And (O, new Muse) gives you the premier place;   11

For that place suits you as does hardness ice,
As liquid waves, and as the heat suits fire,
As light does sun, and loveliness suits Heaven.   14

Sonetto XCV
Risposta

Perche non son, qual mi fai tu, Sirena,
Perche l'almo splendor in me non luce,
Che in te fiammeggia; che la chiara luce
Fora vinta di lui, che'l dì ne mena.   4

Lunge in tutto n'andrei da l'aspra pena,
Che nova doglia al tristo cor m'adduce,
E lieta seguirei te saggio Duce,
La cui virtute ogni mio spirto affrena;   8

Indi repente non che à poco, à poco
Da la mente squarciando il fosco velo
Trà Cigni havrei, qual tu, sublime loco.   11

Sì de gli anni sprezzando il caldo, e'l gielo
Teco ardendo di gloria al nobil foco
Sperar potrei sede beata in Cielo.   14

Sonnet 95
Response (to Ruggieri)

Because I'm not what you'd make me, a siren,
Because life-giving splendor does not light
In me that flames in you; for that bright light
He'd overcome who brings the day to us.   4

In all things, I would flee far from harsh pain,
Which new woe brings me in my woeful heart,
And happily I'd follow you, wise guide,
By whose virtue my every spirit is restrained;   8

Then all at once, not only bit by bit,
While ripping from my mind that gloomy veil;
Like you, midst swans I'd have a lofty place.   11

So through the years, disdaining heat and ice
Aflame with you for glory in noble fire,
I'd hope to find a blessed place in Heaven.   14

Sonetto CII
Del Sig. Arcangelo Zuccaro, Romano

Vostra penna (o stupor) quasi scarpello
Nel sen del Tempo eterno Tempio face,
E se non volge in se suo dente edace,
Fia sempre il loco à meraviglia bello.   4

Atterrò ben questo Colosso, e quello
Doglia apportando à l'Indo, al Perso, al Trace:
Ma vedrem hor del suo poter fallace
La forza, e vinto il pensier crudo, e fello.   8

La salda base de l'egregio stile
Sosterrà le Colonne, e l'aureo Tetto
Di cui fia pompa, e fregio il nome vostro.   11

Si farassi per voi, spirto gentile,
Spirto per adornar la terra eletto,
Con le sfere immortale il secol nostra.   14

Sonnet 102
By Mr. Archangelo Zuccaro, the Roman[15]

Your pen (a wonder), almost a chisel's edge,
In time's breast an eternal temple makes;
That place, if on himself his teeth that crush
Time turns not, will forever make a marvel fair.   4

Even the Colossus tumbled down; that[16]
Sorrow was felt from the Indus to Persia to Thrace.
But now we'll try the strength of Time's false power,
For foiled has been his planning, cruel and fell.   8

The solid base of your distinguished style
Will shore the columns, prop the golden roof
That will embellish and adorn your name.   11

Yes it will be for you, O noble soul,
To grace the earth with beauty, soul elect—
Grace, with the immortal spheres, this age of ours.   14

Sonetto CIII
Risposta

Stemprata è la mia penna, e lo scarpello
De l'ingegno destrutto, ond'hor ben face
Preda infelice il crudo Tempo edace
D'ogni mio studio nel fiorir più bello: 4

Ma sia che può; s'ei non renova quello
In me, che à Filomena il fiero Trace
Spietato fece, il suo poter fallace
Vedrassi, e vinto l'empio orgoglio, e fello.   8

Con brevi note il pellegrino stile
Loderò suo malgrado, e l'humil tetto
Dal cor sia nido al chiaro nome vostro.   11

Al nome, per cui già l'alma gentile
Veggio farsi, e cantar che al Mondo eletto
Foste, per far eterno il secol nostro.   14

Sonnet 103
Response (to Zucarro)

My pen's point has grown dull, my chisel's edge
Devoid of wit, whence now indeed Time makes
Unhappy prey, for cruel Time will crush
My every work when most it's blooming fair.   4

But come what may; if he does not do that
To me which Philomena suffered from fierce Thrace[17]
Unmercifully wronged, Time's power false
We'll test and overcome—his fell and wicked pride.   8

With notes succinct the rare and novel style
I'll praise despite his will; let the low roof
Of my heart be a nest for your bright name.   11

To that name, by which I surely see the soul
Ennobled, [I hear] sung that in this world
To make our age immortal you've been picked.   14

Sonetto CIV
Del Sig. Agostin Gioioso da Sanseverino

Comica illustre, il cui saper, e l'arte
Europa tutta, e l'Universo honora:
Mentre d'alto Teatro odo talhora
Il tuo dir, ò l'ammiro in dotte carte,   4

Dico: "Thalia da Pindo in questa parte
Scesa co'l foco d'oro, e'l sen di Flora
Parla divinamente, e seco ancora
Hà de le sue sorelle ogni altra parte.   8

"La voce, la memoria, il suono, il canto,
L'amor, gloria ed i celesti honori
D'Urania, doni eccelsi d'ISABELLA."   11

Anzi dico: "costei vince di tanto
Le gratie tutte de' Castalii Chori
Quanto il Sol di splendor vince ogni Stella."   14

Sonnet 104
By Mr. Agostin Gioioso da Sanseverino

O famed comedienne, whose name and art
All Europe knows and all the world now honors,
While from the theater high I hear sometimes
Your speech, or read it on your learned page,   4

I say: "Down from Pindus, Thalia to these parts[18]
Has come with golden flame, and the bosom
Of Flora speaks divinely; with her too[19]
She has all of her sisters' other gifts.   8

"The voice, the memory, the sound, the song,
The glory, love, celestial honors rich
Of Urania, lofty gifts of ISABELLA."[20]   11

I rather say: "She outshines just as far
Every grace of the Castalian choir[21]
As the sun's splendor vanquishes each star."   14

Sonetto CV
Risposta

Se'l raro stil, se la mirabil arte,
Che Pindo, il Mondo, e'l Ciel orna, & honora,
Se i dolci carmi suoi miro talhora,
Anzi le gemme, ond'hor fregi le carte;   4

Dico: "nè in quella fortunata parte
Dove è più illustre il Pò, nè in grembo à Flora
Nè in altra (s'altra è più famosa) ancora
Hebbe cigno qual tù lodata parte.   8

"SENNA, c'hor ode il tuo soave canto
Non invidia al Patolo i ricchi honori:"
Canta, che da l'oblio tragge ISABELLA.   11

"Spirto gentil tù pur passi di tanto
Il merto mio, quanto gli Empirei Chori
Passan d'altezza l'amorosa Stella."   14

Sonnet 105
Response (to Gioioso)

If that rare style and if the marvelous art
That graces Pindus, and the world with honor,
Heaven too; and if his sweet songs I sometimes
Admire—his gems instead—whence now you mark the page,   4

I say this: "Neither in those favored parts
Where the Po's most famed, nor in Flora's bosom,
Nor elsewhere (if elsewhere enjoys more fame)
Could one find a swan endowed with all your gifts.[22]   8

"The river SEINE that hears your dulcet song
Does not begrudge now Patolus' honors rich."[23]
I'll sing, for from oblivion song saves ISABELLA: 11

"Noble spirit, you surpass as far
My merit as the high empyrean choir
Exceeds the height of Venus's amorous star."   14

Notes

1. *Thetis*: a sea nymph, daughter of Proteus, the old man of the sea.

2. *these . . . those*: in the caves or under the cloud. The Italian adjective *Cimerie*, here translated as "Avernan" can either allude to the cave of the Sybil at Lake Avernus near Naples or to caves in countries in the Balkans or the Middle East.

3. *life-giving jewel*: The moon; Renaissance astronomical theory held that starlight was reflected moonlight.

4. *lucky shepherd*: Endymion—a Latmian shepherd who made love to the moon in exchange for a fleece of wool.

5. *Marini*: playwright Giovan Battista Marini (1569-1625), one of the most celebrated lyric poets of his age, praised Andreini's performance of the character Apollo in one of his interludes.

6. *breath away*: The Italian literally says "Curbs my every spirit." The vital spirits were thought by Renaissance medicine to be responsible for the bodily motions and functions—among which, of course, respiring. When something made one catch one's breath, the spirits were thought to have momentarily suspended their coursing through the body.

7. *Lethe's depths*: One of the rivers of the underworld, Lethe's waters make the dead forget everything. Time curses works that cannot be forgotten and outlast him.

8. *conqueror of the world*: In her role of Apollo in Marini's play, Andreini is the world's conqueror.

9. *most Christian*: This phrase was a hereditary title of French royalty.

10. *golden age*: The Italian literally says of the "primal age," which was the age of gold.

11. *Sincero*: Jacopo Sannazaro, also known as Sincero (1458-1530) was a celebrated poet in his time.

12. *Sebeto*: The small Campagnian stream on which the city of Naples is situated.

13. *Lucifer . . . Hesperus*: Lucifer is the morning star—Venus. Hesperus is the evening star—also Venus.

14. *Bactrus . . . Thule*: The Bactrus is a river, now named the Dehas, in Central Asia. Thule: either the island of Mainland in the Shetlands or Iceland.

15. *Zuccarro*: Federigo Zuccarri or Zuccarro (1502 or 1503-1609) was a portrait painter of international renown who founded the Academy of St. Luke in Rome and became its first president.

16. *Colossus*: A statue that stood astride the entrance to the harbor at Rhodes. One of the seven wonders of the ancient world.

17. *Filomena* . . . Thrace: Filomena, a sister of Queen Procne of Thrace, was raped by her brother-in-law, King Terreus, who then cut out her tongue and imprisoned her in a tower. Unless Andreini should lose her tongue, she plans to keep writing songs and singing.

18. *Pindus*: A mountain in Thessaly on the border of Macedonia. Pindus was thought to be the seat of the Muses. Thalia: The muse of comedy.

19. *Flora*: Old Italian deity of fertility and flowers. She had a temple in Rome and also is associated with Florence.

20. *Urania*: The muse of astronomy.

21. *Castalian choir*: All the Muses together. The epithet derives from a spring, sacred to the Muses, into which the nymph Castalia threw herself when pursued by Apollo.

22. *swan*: a poet.

23. *Patolus*: A river sometimes associated with the Greek poet Pindar.

Index of First Lines

A che piango infelice? à che sospiro?... 52
A che sguardi amorosetti 90
A l'apparir del Sole.. 64
A le rose, che in Cielo apre l'Aurora,.. 174
Alma, ch'al Ciel salita 106
Amor d'amor ardea.. 66
Amor se con leggiadro, e novo inganno 90
Amorosa mia Clori 98
Anima stanca à che sospiri, e piagni?... 128
Avara, liberal, cruda, e pietosa 176
Care gemme d'Apollo onde il mio giorno 172
Care gioie, Che le noie... 86
Chi pensò mai veder fra terra oscura 114
Colma di fasto io me ne gia cantando,.. 184
Comica illustre, il cui saper, e l'arte 204
Con lagrime di sangue, e con sospiri 132
Con quai giri lascivetti... 118
De la mia bella Donna 120
Deh girate, Luci amate.. 98
Del sereno mio Sol la chiara luce 50
Di sdegnoso rossor Febo t'accendi 166
Dimmi, lasso mio core,.. 186
Donna se voi poteste... 122
Dopo la pioggia del mio pianto amaro... 78
È Danza, ò pugna questa? ecco s'io miro 174
È Spento il foco, è spento, ... 128
Ecco l'Alba rugiadosa.. 44
Faccia al gran Marte risonar le 'ncudi 46

Fuor de l'onde trahea sereno il giorno 180
Già vidi occhi leggiadri, occhi, ond'Amore.. 54
Hor che 'l dotto Sincero estinto giace,... 186
Hor che la Notte à la suprema altezza
     (Incantesimo egloga III) 148
Hor che strale d'Amor più non m'offende;.. 142
Hor qual grave per l'aria odo lamento? 134
Il mio vago homicida.. 40
In ischietto vestir vera bellezza,... 188
In leggiadretta gonna, ... 116
In questo c'hor t'invio 174
In saldissimo gielo 176
Io credeà, che trà gli amanti.. 80
Io t' amo, e ti desìo;... 96
Io vissi un tempo (ond' hor meco mi sdegno) 146
La tua gran Musa hor che non può? quand'ella 138
Languisco, e son tant'anni 122
Le perle già di rugiadoso humore 38
Lunge da le tue luci alme, e divine.. 68
Mentre quasi liquor tutto bollente... 60
Misera pria sarà calda la neve,.. 64
Morfeo gentil se nel mostrarmi solo 62
Morrò crudel, morrò, ma nel morire 168
Moveà dolce un zefiretto 122
Nel giorno, che sublime in bassi manti... 136
O Bellissimo petto 84
O De l'anima mia nobil tesoro.. 58
O Di Pianta Real vago, e sublime 178
O Lagrime, ch'ad arte.. 76
O Mia Nisa, ò mio cor mentr'io vagheggio 114
O Non men crudo, e rio, che bello, e vago 36
Ove sì tosto voli.. 120
Ove trà vaghi fior nascosto è l'Angue 102
Per fuggir la prigione,.. 130
Per lo soverchio affanno 56
Per pietà di me stesso... 116

Perche non son, qual mi fai tu, Sirena, ... 198
Porta la Donna mia 116
Qual candida Colomba 146
Qual dispietato artiglio il cor mi svelle? 168
Qual Ruscello veggiam d'acque sovente 32
Qual travagliata Nave io mi raggìro 68
Qualhor candida, e vaga 96
Qualhor miro l'argento 168
Quando alluma nascendo il Sol la terra, ... 78
Quando sdegno gli sproni aspri, e pungenti 56
Quanti trofèi già d'arme vaga, e quanti 112
Quella bocca di rose 130
Quest'empia Donna altera, ... 62
S' Alcun sia mai, che i versi miei negletti 30
S'a la vostra armonia bella Sirena, ... 196
Se 'l raro stil, se la mirabil arte, ... 206
Se da le Sfere, onde 'l valor prendeste 84
Se in nobil Donna angelici sembianti, ... 192
Se per quelli salvar, ch'errar vedesti, ... 140
Sgombra dal ciglio homai gli amari pianti 194
Sgombra, sgombra da te mio tristo core 144
Spettator del mio mal, son hoggi intento 170
Spirando l'aure placide, e seconde 34
Standomi dietro ad una quercia antica 130
Stemprata è la mia penna, e lo scarpello 202
Tirsi dolce mio ben se dal valore, ... 76
Trà questi duri sassi 112
Tu con leggiadra insolita vaghezza 182
Un bel sembiante in habito negletto 190
Va pur lasso mio core 90
Vago di posseder l'indico argento, ... 40
Vide Lesbin Nisida sua fugace 86
Vostra penna (o stupor) quasi scarpello 200

About the Editor and Translator

Anne MacNeil is a fellow of the American Academy in Rome and the American Association of University Women and currently holds a faculty appointment at the University of North Carolina at Chapel Hill. Professor MacNeil received her Ph.D. in the history and theory of music from the University of Chicago, where she studied with the late Howard Mayer Brown. She has published articles on Isabella Andreini and her family in the *Journal of the Royal Musical Association*, the *Musical Quarterly*, *Early Music*, *Renaissance Studies*, and the *New Grove Dictionary of Music and Musicians*. Her book, *Music and Women of the Commedia dell'Arte in the Late Sixteenth Century* (2003), is published by Oxford University Press.

James Wyatt Cook is Langbo Trustees' professor emeritus at Albion College. His verse translations include *Petrarch's Songbook: Rerum vulgarium fragmenta* and *The Autobiography of Lorenzo de' Medici: A Commentary on My Sonnets*, both published by the Center for Medieval and Renaissance Texts and Studies; and *Florentine Drama for Convent and Festival: Seven Sacred Plays* by Antonia Pulci, published by the University of Chicago Press. Cook is currently preparing the *Facts on File Encyclopedia of Renaissance Literature*. He has been a research fellow of the British Academy, the Newberry Library, the Pontifical Institute for Medieval Studies, and the Centre for Reformation and Renaissance Studies at the University of Toronto.